Business Ethics

American University Studies

Series V
Philosophy
Vol. 142

PETER LANG
New York • San Francisco • Bern • Baltimore
Frankfurt am Main • Berlin • Wien • Paris

Sherwin Klein

Business Ethics

Reflections from a
Platonic Point of View

PETER LANG
New York • San Francisco • Bern • Baltimore
Frankfurt am Main • Berlin • Wien • Paris

Library of Congress Cataloging-in-Publication Data

Klein, Sherwin.
    Business ethics: reflections from a Platonic point of view /
Sherwin Klein.
        p.   cm.
    Includes bibliographical references and index.
    1. Business ethics—United States.   2. Ethics.   I. Title.
    HF5387.K575   1993   174'.4—dc20   92-22662
    ISBN 0-8204-1948-6   CIP
    ISSN 0739-6392

Die Deutsche Bibliothek-CIP-Einheitsaufnahme

Klein, Sherwin:
Business ethics : reflections from a Platonic point of view /
Sherwin Klein. - New York; Bern; Berlin; Frankfurt/M.; Paris;
Wien: Lang, 1993
    (American university studies : Ser. 5, Philosophy;   Vol. 142)
    ISBN 0-8204-1948-6
NE: American university studies/05

The paper in this book meets the guidelines for permanence and
durability of the Committee on Production Guidelines for
Book Longevity of the Council on Library Resources.

© Peter Lang Publishing, Inc., New York 1993

Printed in the United States of America.

To my wife Eleanor and

my sons Chuck and Dave

ACKNOWLEDGEMENTS

A number of people have given me aid, encouragement, and support in writing this book. In particular, I would like to thank the following people: My wife, Eleanor, has been a constant source of support during our marriage, and the writing of this book is no exception. She not only read all the drafts of the manuscript, proofreading all of the chapters and making helpful stylistic improvements, but she was burdened with the proofreading of the original articles from which a substantial portion of this book was taken. My friend Christopher Perricone read the manuscript in its last stages and made many helpful suggestions which improved the book. Anthony Preus, one of Lang's readers, was also very helpful. Guided by some of his suggestions, I reorganized the manuscript and made substantial changes in some of the chapters.

I wish to thank the following editors for allowing me to use portions of my articles which were published in their journals: Robert J. Baum, editor of *Business and Professional Ethics Journal*, Elliot D. Cohen, editor of *International Journal of Applied Philosophy*, and Richard A. Kruse, editor of *Scholar and Educator.* "Is a Moral Organization Possible?" [*Business and Professional Ethics Journal*, vol. 7, #1 (1990): 51–73] appears, with minor revisions, in Appendix I, and "Platonic Virtue Theory and Business Ethics," [*Business and Professional Ethics Journal*, vol. 8, #4 (1990): 59–82] has been used, in a revised form, in Chapter I and Appendix II. "Platonic *Paideia* and Business Statesmanship," [*The International Journal of Applied Philosophy*, vol. 4, #2 (Fall 1988): 63–75] comprises, with some revisions, Chapter 5. Some of my article, "Is Business Ethics a Fiction?" [*Scholar and Educator*, vol. 11, #1 (Spring 1987): 30–36] was used in Appendix I.

My articles, "Two Views of Business Ethics: A Popular Philosophical Approach and A Value Based Interdisciplinary One," [*Journal of Business Ethics*, vol. 4, #1 (February 1985): 71–79], and "Plato's *Statesman* and the Nature of

Business Leadership: An Analysis from an Ethical Point of View," [*Journal of Business Ethics*, vol. 7 (April 1988): 283–294] have been used with the permission of Kluwer Academic Publishers. Ideas from the former article are included in Chapters 1, 2, 3, and 6, and portions of the latter article appear in Chapter 4.

Some of the costs associated with the final stages of preparing the manuscript were defrayed by a grant from Fairleigh Dickinson University. I wish to thank the committee that awarded the grant to me.

CONTENTS

CHAPTER VII   POSTSCRIPT   117

APPENDIX I   IS A MORAL ORGANIZATION POSSIBLE?   125

APPENDIX II   CORPORATE CULTURE AND VIRTUE ETHICS   147

INDEX   155

PREFACE

Many business ethics texts written by philosophers emphasize the application of ethical theory to case studies in business. Normative ethical theories are usually divided into two types, deontological and teleological (or utilitarian), and these theories are applied to moral problems in business for the purpose of determining what one ought to do when faced with these dilemmas. Such an approach seems reasonable, since business leaders will look to business ethics specialists for guidance in solving concrete moral problems that they face in the course of their activities. I attempt to show that although this way of viewing business ethics has validity, it is not without difficulties, and a value-based (and virtue-based) interdisciplinary approach may yield more satisfactory results. This latter form of business ethics relies more on the insights of the ancient Greek philosophers, Plato and Aristotle, than on Kant and the utilitarians.

In my book, I use Plato both to raise serious ethical problems for business and to provide what I believe to be a viable solution to these problems. Thus, as the title suggests, the book consists of reflections from a Platonic point of view on basic ethical problems in business. Although scholars have written articles on business ethics using the insights of ancient Greek philosophers, nothing on the scale of this book, to my knowledge, has been done.

In Chapter 1, I discuss two types of ethical theory with respect to their applicability to business ethics—the use of normative ethical principles (deontological and teleological) in attempting to solve concrete moral problems in business and a more value and virtue-based ethics approach. I show that, in the context of business ethics, the latter type of theory compares quite favorably with the former one, and it directly addresses the most serious concerns of people who are skeptical about the possibility of business ethics. Chapters 2 and 3 are devoted to a discussion of pre and postdepression American business values respectively. I analyze the effects of these values on the character of American businesspeople, and the moral implications of these values are considered in some detail. This analysis, I believe, should help one to understand better the sources of many ethical difficulties that exist today in American business. Chapters 4 and 5 develop a Platonic critique of American business leadership from a character or virtue point of view. In Chapter 4, I use Plato's *Statesman* to show that his model for leadership, the weaving of temperate and courageous qualities in leaders, is a most useful model for analyzing business leadership from an ethical point of view. Moreover, I argue that the history of American business values, in both its pre and postdepression forms, exhibits the ethical difficulties that Plato discusses with considerable clarity in this dialogue. In Chapter 5, I use Plato's conception of *paideia* or education to develop a systematic critique of the dominant values of American business leaders. Emphasis is placed on criticizing business values that are harmful to the human soul and, therefore, undermine the Platonic cardinal virtues—wisdom, courage, temperance, and justice. In Chapter 6, I discuss what I believe to be necessary in order to construct an ethical model for business along Platonic lines. A craftsmanship model of business management is defended. I attempt to show that on its foundation one can construct a business organization that is more ethical than any that is built upon the more traditional American business values. Indeed, I show in some detail how the craftsmanship model answers the more important Platonic criticisms of American business values. Nonetheless, this model incorporates the notion of self-interest—a motive which most businesspeople think underlies the realities of doing business; it does this, however, in a morally propitious way, since a craftsmanship type of self-interest is related to altruism. Chapter 7 is a postscript to the preceding chapter. In this chapter, I argue for the practicality of the craftsmanship model and discuss the difficulties of implementing this ethic in American business.

Philosophers have addressed themselves to the problem of the pessimism concerning the possibility of business ethics. It is generally agreed that the more popular pessimism can be sufficiently defused, but the more philosophical pessimism concerning the possibility of a formal moral organization is more difficult to undermine. Although a discussion of the popular pessimism concerning business ethics appears to be of general interest, the latter problem may hold little interest for readers who are not concerned with more technical, philosophical questions. Therefore, I have placed a discussion of the pessimism concerning the possibility of business ethics in Appendix I. Many contemporary business management theorists are concerned with the notion of corporate culture. For those readers who are interested in this concept, I have included a second appendix in which the concept of corporate culture is discussed from the point of view of virtue.

This book is free of philosophical jargon and does not require a sophisticated understanding of Plato. It was my intention in writing this book to appeal to the reader who has interdisciplinary, and not merely philosophical, business ethics interests and is willing to grapple with problems in this field at a level that has some intellectual depth. Indeed, it is my contention that only an interdisciplinary approach to business ethics can do justice to the subject. It is my hope, therefore, that the book will have a broader appeal than one which is strictly applied philosophy. This latter type of text is preferred by certain philosophers, but such works have sustained criticism from business ethics specialists who believe that the approach is too narrowly philosophical.

There are, I believe, a number of philosophers and people in business management (especially business management theorists who emphasize culture as an essential concept in business ethics) who would welcome a systematically developed value-based business ethic. Laura Nash, a specialist in business ethics, suggests the importance of my approach when she says,

> Every company has values that are expressed through the corporate culture. These values come down from the chief executive. And it is in shaping that culture, in deciding what the company is about, that ethical behavior will or will not be built in.... Business ethics is largely a question of corporate character.[1]

1. Tomar Lewin mentions these remarks in "Business Ethic's New Appeal," *New York Times*, Sunday, December 11, 1983.

CHAPTER I

ETHICAL THEORY AND BUSINESS ETHICS

1. Types of Ethical Theory and Business Ethics

It seems to be a generally accepted view among philosophers who write business ethics texts that some knowledge of ethical theory is necessary in order to do such applied ethics adequately. Since this position has merit, in this chapter I shall consider types of ethical theory and discuss their applicability to business.

It is a commonplace of contemporary moral theory to divide normative ethics into two types, teleological and deontological. Both of these theories attempt to answer the question: what ought I to do? Therefore, their object is actions rather than agents. The teleologist believes that the rightness or wrongness of actions is determined by their consequences. Thus, they are also called consequentialists. The most common teleological moral theory is utilitarianism.[1] Utilitarian moral theory emphasizes the concept of good, and what is right, according to classical utilitarians, is determined by that which is productive of the greatest amount of good. That is, what is considered right is what leads to actions that, on balance, yield more good consequences than bad ones.[2]

Utilitarians disagree about the nature of intrinsic goodness. Some utilitarians are hedonists and thus equate the human good or happiness with pleasure and the avoidance of pain. Other utilitarians believe that pleasure is not the only intrinsic good; goods such as knowledge and friendship may have equal or greater intrinsic value. A problem arises, however, concerning how these intrinsic goods are to be determined and ranked. But even amongst hedonistic utilitarians there is disagreement about criteria for applying the utilitarian principle. Jeremy Bentham maintains that quantitative determinations alone should be used to evaluate pleasures and pains (pleasures and pains are to be evaluated by the following criteria: intensity, duration, certainty or uncertainty, propinquity or remoteness, fecundity, purity, and extent), while John Stuart Mill argues that qualitative differences, distinctions between higher and lower pleasures (pleasures relating to higher and lower faculties), are most relevant in determining happiness.

Modern utilitarians distinguish between act and rule utilitarianism. Act utilitarians believe that the rightness or wrongness of an action should be determined by the good or bad consequences of individual actions in specific circumstances. Rule utilitarians, however, believe that the rightness and wrongness of actions should be judged by the good and bad consequences of justifiable rules governing types of actions. It is important to note that these two theories can lead to conflicting moral judgments. An act utilitarian may agree that generally we ought not to break our promises, but maintain that in some specific circumstance(s) the good consequences accruing to breaking a promise outweigh the bad.[3] Rule utilitarians, however, would maintain that even if this were the case, the rule applying to promise keeping should be followed (assuming no contrary, justifiable moral rule applies to the circumstance), for general adherence to justifiable moral rules will maximize that which is good.[4]

Opponents of utilitarianism have argued that there can be examples of actions which, on balance, yield more good than bad consequences, but the actions offend our sense of justice. It may be possible, for example, to invent a scenario in which injustice to some minority maximizes happiness. Whatever the consequences, our sense of justice would cause us to condemn such an action.[5] The objection can also be phrased in terms of the violation of this minority's rights. Deprivation of rights, it may be argued, cannot be justified by showing that good has been maximized. Since the deontologist places the emphasis on doing what is right or just for its own sake, it would seem that the deontologist, and not the utilitarian, best captures our intuitive sense of justice. Let us, then, consider their position.

In contrast to the teleologist, the deontologist believes that right (or duty or moral obligation), rather than good consequences, is the fundamental moral concept. That which is right (our duty or moral obligation) ought to be done simply because it is the right thing to do or is our duty. That is, an action is right (one's duty or moral obligation) if it is an example of a certain kind, e.g., telling the truth or keeping one's promise. Immanuel Kant's deontological moral theory has been the most influential.[6] For Kant, a moral action is done solely from the moral motive—to do one's duty simply because it is one's duty. Morally permissible acts can be determined by applying the categorical imperative. Kant believes that given the (subjective) principle of any proposed action (maxim), one should ask (on one formulation of the categorical imperative), can we will the maxim to be a universal law of nature?[7] According to Kant, morally impermissible actions can be shown to be inconsistent once they are universalized in the above manner. For example, he suggests that if I intend to borrow money without the prospect of paying it back, and I attempt to universalize this position, I will see that I cannot consistently do it, for no one would consider that a promise was actually made. Generally, a person who commits immoral acts wants to make himself or herself an exception. One way of looking at this notion of violating the categorical imperative is to note that the immoral person probably would not want done to him what he wishes to do to others. But to act morally, according to Kant, one must be willing to universalize the principles of one's proposed actions, and this entails the above notion of reversibility. It is difficult to state accurately the principle of a proposed action that one is to test. With enough ingenuity, an immoral person can state a maxim specifically enough to invalidate Kant's test. It is necessary, then, to formulate a maxim honestly, rather than to attempt to find loopholes in Kant's method. As Kant says, a moral person acts from a good will.

At best, the categorical imperative determines what not to do, but the class of permissible actions is not identical with the class of actions that are obligatory (our duty). A Kantian could agree but argue that the categorical imperative can show that it is wrong *not* to do certain actions and, therefore, determine some actions to be obligatory. But critics have argued that Kant's test does not adequately delimit the class of actions which ought not to be done. Some actions apparently supported by the categorical imperative should not be done, and some rejected by the test should be done. Critics have argued that consistent immoralists are possible. A sincere Nazi could believe in abhorrent principles such as the right to persecute Jews and consistently apply the categorical imperative. A businessperson who sincerely believes in extreme dog-eat-dog competition could consistently apply the categorical imperative to principles of proposed actions that would generally be considered immoral. Critics have also argued that Kant takes a too rigid view of exceptions to rules. If, as Kant thought, the categorical imperative forbids lying under any circumstances, we would be forbidden to do so even if, for example, a lie would prevent a murder. Thus, it would seem, we would be forbidden to do something we ought to do.[8] A similar problem arises when we consider conflicts of duty. Moral dilemmas for businesspeople can take the form of conflicts of duty, but some critics have argued that Kant's method for determining permissible actions is not very helpful for reconciling conflicts of duty. Thus, for example, if we are forbidden to tell lies, but the categorical imperative also supports the preservation of innocent lives, such a conflict of duty cannot be resolved by Kant's test. But the inability of his test to resolve such a conflict of duty can be construed as preventing us from doing what apparently we should do in this situation, viz., tell a lie. Apart from the problem of conflicts of duty, there may be actions which the categorical imperative determines ought not to be done which are not only permissible; they are laudatory. Certain generally recognized goods such as self-sacrifice could not be universalized; if everyone is self-sacrificing, who is left to accept this action?

Kant also presents a more concrete version of the categorical imperative, one which is often thought to be particularly helpful. He thinks that moral action entails treating human beings as having intrinsic value (inherent dignity); therefore, it is never moral to use people as means to further one's own private ends. But as valuable as this principle is, there can be an honest difference of opinion concerning whether or not some proposed action does treat a person as a means to an end in some objectionable sense.[9]

In recent years some moral philosophers have argued for a return to what has been called virtue ethics. These virtue ethics theorists, in the main, take their inspiration from ancient Greek philosophers, especially Aristotle. This movement is often traced back to works by G. E. M. Anscombe and Philippa Foot.[10] They attempt to make virtue (excellence of character) and vice, and therefore the agent, basic to moral theory rather than the intrinsic rightness of, or morally good consequences of, actions. However, Alasdair MacIntyre (*After Virtue*) is the most influential virtue ethics theorist.

MacIntyre, Anscombe, and Foot take a neoAristotelian approach to virtue ethics rather than the Platonic position taken in this book. One should note, however, that virtue ethics has its source in the practical philosophy of Plato and was developed by his student, Aristotle. A virtue is a human excellence and, according to MacIntyre, for traditions as different as the Aristotelian (and I would include Platonic) and Christian, a virtue is a human excellence because it is essential for achieving the human good.[11] Of course, putative virtues will differ if, as in the above case, the concepts of the human good differ, but the concept of virtue remains the same. This notion of virtue entails that for X to be a real virtue, the human good that it attempts to achieve must be a real human good. Thus, a basic premise regulating Socratic inquiry is the belief that virtue is a good and, therefore, is always beneficial. If a virtue is always beneficial, it must be a benefit (a good) for both the possessor of the virtue and for those people who are affected by the virtuous conduct.[12]

If, as I believe, some knowledge of ethical theory is necessary in order to deal intelligently with moral problems in corporate business, it is important to consider which type(s) of ethical theory is most helpful in this context. In this regard, the distinction between action-based theories (utilitarian and deontological) and virtue-based theories should prove to be helpful.

People generally, and certainly businesspeople, assume that if ethical theory is to be helpful, it should provide the tools or method(s) for determining what we ought to do when faced with moral dilemmas. It would seem, however, that a virtue-based ethic, since it is agent rather than action-oriented, is ill-equipped to solve the moral problems in business; business leaders look to business ethics specialists for guidance in solving problems concerning what they ought to do about perceived moral problems, i.e., action-based problems. It would appear, then, that we ought to look to a principle and/or rule-oriented ethic, viz., a utilitarian or deontological ethic, rather than a virtue ethic, to solve the perceived moral dilemmas of businesspeople.[13]

Whether such a criticism of the use of a virtue-based ethic is implicit in the approach taken by many business ethics authors, it is clear that those texts which include a chapter(s) on ethical theory emphasize action-based, rather than agent-based, theories. Discussions of normative ethical theory almost invariably begin by dividing such theories into teleological (or consequentialist) and deontological (or nonconsequentialist) theories, and some difficulties in these theories are considered.[14] The use of such theories can provide the student with an understanding of philosophically clarified moral rules and/or principles and, therefore, with tools for analyzing moral problems. Such analyses could help to develop one's sensitivity to the complexity of moral problems in business, and possibly increase one's skill at working out for oneself solutions to some of these problems. It should be noted, however, that a course taught along these lines can tend, basically, to be a simplified ethics course applied to some business problems. Business ethics instructors who take this approach would have to agree with Peter F. Drucker[15] who argues that there is no separate ethics for business, nor is it necessary to have one. Moreover, the question of which sort of approach to ethics, ancient Greek or modern, best sensitizes people to the complexity of moral problems ought to be considered. If an important purpose of moral education is to sensitize young people to the moral dimensions of life, it would seem that more emphasis should be placed on developing excellences of character rather than solving moral puzzles. Moral problems are understood most clearly by people of good character; without good character, it is difficult to see how one could persuade a person to accept certain problems as moral problems. One may also point out a difficulty in attempting to solve problems by appealing to alternative action-based ethical theories. These theories sensitize one to see problems in terms of the theories. Thus, for example, moral problems for a utilitarian are viewed solely from the standpoint of the greatest happiness principle. Similarly, a Kantian sees moral problems solely from the standpoint of determining what duty requires. If this is the case, in what sense, for example, can utilitarians and Kantians be said to be dealing with the same moral problems? Don't their particular perspectives narrow their perception of moral problems?

There is another issue that ought to be raised with respect to how one ought to approach moral problems generally. Edmund L. Pincoffs has argued that contemporary ethical theorists (utilitarians and deontologists) agree that ethics seeks to find methods, principles, and rules for solving moral problems. He calls this "quandary ethics."[16] We have seen that business leaders would approve of this view of ethics, and I will have more to say on this topic in the next section. The ancient Greek philosophers Plato and Aristotle, however, take a different approach to ethics. The purpose of ethics is to determine the good life (*eudaimonia*) and those qualities of character necessary to lead such a life. As Pincoffs says, Aristotle was more concerned with how not to fall into moral traps than in solving moral problems;[17] this is equally true of Plato. To use Pincoff's terms, they are more concerned with preventative than curative medicine; the emphasis is on moral health, not curing diseases. Although curative medicine certainly has its place in business ethics, it would be foolish to deny the validity of the Aristotelian and Platonic approach to moral health.

In order to deal intelligently with moral problems in corporate business, it is necessary to be sensitive to the complexities of moral issues and to possess sound moral judgment. I have argued that character education is more effective in sensitizing people to moral concerns than teaching people to use modern ethical theories to solve moral puzzles. One may also argue that character education is most essential in developing sound moral judgment, but this aspect of ethics is neglected by modern ethical theorists.

In either of the two types of normative ethical theory discussed above, virtue is handmaiden to another (central) moral concept; that is, in utilitarianism, it is a disposition to produce the greatest possible good and in deontological moral theory, it is a disposition to do what is morally right or our moral duty. In both cases, the concept of virtue is unduly narrowed; moral virtue is equated with either benevolence or conscientiousness. Moreover, from a discussion of modern ethical theory, one may get the impression that sound moral judgment is based upon either the capacity to determine consequences that maximize happiness or properly applying a fundamental moral principle such as the categorical imperative for determining what is morally wrong. But how can one have sound moral judgment without possessing good character? The quality of a person's moral judgments is based upon the quality of a person's character. This, of course, is not to deny that knowledge of relevant facts and careful determination of the consequences that follow from proposed actions is necessary. Rather, my claim is that moral character and reasoning are intimately related.[18] MacIntyre agrees and suggests that when Aristotle argues that excellence of character and intelligence are inseparable

(*Nicomachean Ethics* 1144a37), he is presenting "a view characteristically at odds with that dominant in the modern world."[19]

If, as many writers on business ethics suggest, normative ethical theories are the tools to be used in practicing business ethics, it is important, for the purpose of business ethics, to determine conditions for their proper use. A major purpose of my all-too-brief survey of normative ethical theories is to raise questions about their proper use.[20] There are a sufficient number of serious difficulties with both utilitarian and Kantian theories to suggest that business ethicists who rely on one or the other or both of these theories, but do not adequately address the difficulties, are doing business ethics from a superficial foundation. Moreover, how does one determine when to use one or the other or both of these normative ethical theories? When do utilitarian claims override deontological ones or vice versa? What principle(s) should we use to solve such problems? Clearly, although at least philosophers who do business ethics are aware of these problems, there is no consensus among business ethics theorists on how to answer these questions. For example, William J. Blackstone ("Reverse Discrimination and Compensatory Justice") and Tom L. Beauchamp ("The Justification of Reverse Discrimination in Hiring") take opposite positions, nonutilitarian verses utilitarian, on the moral problem of reverse discrimination.[21]

Second, we have seen that there is considerable disagreement among utilitarians concerning the nature of a sound utilitarian theory. Therefore, not only may utilitarian and Kantian theories lead to different ethical conclusions, but different utilitarian theories, as was suggested, could lead to conflicting moral judgments. It would seem, then, that an adequate use of any version of these theories requires more than the relatively simple discussions one finds in many business ethics texts.

Finally, business ethicists who use normative ethical theories should discuss the limits of their use. Some of the most talked about ethical dilemmas in business, e.g., the problem of whistle blowing, are extremely difficult to solve by applying the above traditional normative ethical theories.

Many American and British moral philosophers of the second half of this century practice what has been called metaethics rather than normative ethics. Metaethics is generally conceived to have two parts: a conceptual analysis of key ethical terms and a search for a correct method of moral reasoning. R. M. Hare, one of the most popular exponents of this view, argues for the connection between metaethics and applied ethics.

> I entered moral philosophy, and indeed philosophy itself, because I was confronted (as I still am) with serious moral questions, and wanted to answer them in a rational manner.... However, I did not trust myself at that early time to publish much on practical issues, because I was not so confident then as I am now that I had a theory of moral reasoning that would withstand scrutiny. Without such a theory, whatever one writes on practical issues is bound to be insecure.[22]

Some philosophers question whether such a project is necessary in order to consider adequately questions in business ethics. However, even if, for the sake of argument, we accept Hare's position, we need not share his confidence in his method of reasoning. Many philosophers, including myself, have difficulty accepting his method. Nor has the rival method of John Rawls, reflective equilibrium, escaped justified criticism. This is not the place to engage in a lengthy criticism of their positions.[23] It suffices for my purpose to note that there is nothing near consensus concerning the validity of their methods. Therefore, it would appear to be premature to rely on these methods to solve the ethical problems of businesspeople. But are there any methods of ethical reasoning upon which one can rely? A serious question exists concerning whether a correct method of ethical reasoning can be discovered. Moreover, not only do philosophers disagree about whether such a method is possible, those who believe that an adequate method can be determined, as suggested above, do not agree as to what this method is.

I have considered difficulties in the standard use of ethical theory in business ethics and have compared the approaches of modern ethical theory and ancient Greek ethics with respect to certain important issues because I believe that, in the context of business ethics, thinkers who do business ethics have too often assumed that modern ethical theory is superior to virtue ethics and is adequate for solving the important problems in this area. More will be said about the value of virtue theory for business ethics in the next section.

2. The Place of Two Approaches to Ethical Theory in Business Ethics

It is a philosophical platitude to maintain that since every solution relates to some problem, the basic problem(s) in some area must be understood and clarified before proper solutions can be forthcoming. If we apply this to business ethics, we will observe that two related, although separate, problems must be distinguished (I shall label these problems P1 and P2 respectively). This distinction will help us to provide a place in business ethics for the virtue ethics approach.

(P1) Much of what is written about business ethics by philosophers seems to presuppose morally conscientious business people who are faced with moral problems in their business activities and want to determine what they morally ought or ought not to do (or what is morally right or wrong). As conscientious corporate executives, they are concerned with their moral or social responsibilities with respect to employees, shareholders, consumers, and society in general. From the standpoint of employees, conscientious businesspeople want to know what are their rights and duties, e.g., is whistle blowing morally defensible or even obligatory and if so, in what context(s)? Examples of more specific questions are: Is preferential hiring (or promotion) ever morally justifiable, e.g., to reach affirmative action goals? What constitutes morally responsible conduct in advertising, and with whom does the primary moral responsibility lie?

(P2) There has been a good deal of concern in recent years about business ethics as is shown by the number of seminars, lectures, courses, and the great amount of material that has been written on the subject. Although part of this concern can be traced to the desire of morally conscientious businesspeople for aid in solving business problems that have serious moral implications, the greater part of this concern is related to the widespread belief that amorality, if not immorality, is too prevalent in business. (See Appendix I for a discussion of this problem.) If this is true, a major problem in business ethics is to determine where to look for the sources of business amorality and immorality (as well as business morality), and to discover how business can be made as morally respectable an institution as possible. It should be noted that if this problem can be solved, there will not only be fewer but more likely less complex moral dilemmas to tax the ingenuity of our moral reasoning.

As I show in Appendix I, the popular pessimism about business morality neglects the moral foundation of proper business practice, emphasizes the effects of the narrow economics-oriented business view rather than one which places profit in its proper place, and overemphasizes the putative materialism of businesspeople. Nonetheless, there are substantial negative moral implications of American business values that require examination. Many of the complaints of businesspeople reflect these negative moral implications. Employees complain about employer manipulation and lack of concern for their development and well-being. The employee, they argue, is just another piece of dispensable machinery to be motivated as if he were a Pavlovian dog by the carrot and the stick. The corporate atmosphere is said to be devoid of the truly human element—love and kindness are considered soft and human feelings are discounted. Thus, Roger M. D'Aprix maintains that corporations have no souls.[24] Consumers complain about the low quality that is engineered into products and how some are unsafe and misrepresented. The public, generally, is inundated with stories about white collar business crime, business kickbacks and bribes, pollution of the environment by business, and the like. Employers, themselves, have their own complaints. They point to business thefts, e.g., of trade secrets, not to mention employee goofing-off on the job and general dishonesty.

Contemporary moral philosophers are, in the main, nurtured by modern ethical and metaethical theories rather than ancient Greek ethics. Normative ethical theory (utilitarian and deontological) and metaethics, as we saw, provide the contemporary philosopher with methods, principles, and rules for solving concrete moral problems. As Pincoff says, they do "quandary ethics." Thus, contemporary philosophers who concern themselves with business ethics are most at home with the P1 approach. It is also important to note that many contemporary philosophers are analytic philosophers. They do not usually consider philosophical problems in the holistic manner of the traditional philosopher. Unlike traditional philosophers, analytic philosophers have been trained to deal with philosophical problems in a more piecemeal way. On this view, the value of the philosopher is his or her ability to construct arguments which solve specific philosophical problems.

In an odd way, then, the traditions of American business, on the one hand, and analytic philosophy and modern ethical theory, on the other, converge. We can see this more clearly if we reflect on American business traditions.

Traditional business's bias toward economic considerations and against broad-based intellectual concerns is manifested in the reduction of the rational drive for knowledge to a desire for determining values that are instrumental rather than intrinsic. The traditional American businessperson assumes that our basic values are economic and, therefore, the business intellect should determine the means that best serve economic goals. The frontier ethic, inherited by the robber barons, influenced traditional business thinking; it stresses the ability to find the expedient way to solve the practical problems of life, i.e., yankee know-how, can do, or having smarts. The inventor, not the philosopher, is the model of the "smart" person. The emphasis on efficiency, economy, and expediency tend to blind businesspeople to the need for careful reflection on what has intrinsic value. Possibly, the often criticized emphasis of business on short-term profits, which certainly has unjust consequences, is, in part, a manifestation of the above bias concerning human intelligence. Such a bias would cause one to stress solutions to immediate problems and the consequent immediate rewards that accrue from such solutions.

Given the above analysis, it is clear why many businesspeople would refuse to view the ethical problems of a business as consequences of the value system of the firm as a whole; problem solving in business is not usually directed to the broad-based values or presuppositions of a firm. Therefore, it is natural for businesspeople who are concerned with ethical business dilemmas to view such problems in a piecemeal way and to search for a specific fix for each of these specific problems. No wonder businesspeople insist on a case study approach. Although this approach has value, businesspeople do not necessarily emphasize it for the right reasons.

One may note that just as the attitudes of traditional businesspeople, on the one hand, and analytic philosophers and modern ethical theorists, on the other, tend to converge, so do those of the traditional philosopher who finds his or her inspiration in classical Greek moral theory and those contemporary business management theorists who emphasize the notion of corporate culture. For those readers who are interested in the connection between corporate culture and virtue ethics, see Appendix II.

Virtue ethics is of considerable value in understanding and solving P2 problems. Indeed, in this context I think that this approach is indispensable. If one wishes to evaluate actions morally, one could possibly use the principles of modern ethical theory; but if one wishes to explain the widespread moral concern about business, the most natural way to do this is to use the language of virtue and vice. Thus, for example, if Plato wants to explain the decay of a city, he points to such phenomena as the injustice of a tyrant or the intemperance or cowardice of the citizens. Similarly, the health of a city is explained in terms of the corresponding virtues. Insofar as the P2 problem propelled business ethics into the limelight, it is important to understand that it is virtue ethics rather than modern ethical theory that offers the most natural approach to both an understanding of and solution to the deeper moral problems of business.

We have seen that, for Plato, if X is a real virtue (a human excellence), it is essential for achieving the truly human good. If a real virtue is tied to a truly human good, Plato would argue, as a corollary of this, that the moral deficiencies (vices) of members of an organization are, in part, a result of the inadequate values that guide the organization; that is, the top management of the organization lacks the essential virtue—wisdom. The basic values that guide an organization help to mold the character of the people in the firm (by nurturing certain habits). Therefore, if these values have immoral consequences, the moral character of the people in the organization, and the judgments and activities that result from their character, to that extent, would tend to be corrupted. Moral virtue (and vice) and organizational values are, therefore, intimately connected. Isn't it because the goal of some businesses is thought to be too materialistic that they are called amoral or immoral and the character of businesspeople who manage these firms is thought to be corrupt? Similarly, in the *Republic*, Plato implicitly and explicitly argues that materialism undermines virtue and is the source of many of our moral ills. If one's value system is essentially materialistic, it encourages us to cheat, lie, steal, and the like, for if we can get away with such actions, we will be materialistically better off. It is not surprising, then, that, in the *Republic*, fear of punishment and concern for rewards (Cephalus) is basic to conventional morality, and Thrasymachus argues that if we have the brains and "courage" to do immoral acts in a big way—clothed, as Glaucon says, in the appearance of justice—it is difficult to see why we should not be immoral. Is this not a basic problem for people who hold powerful positions in organizations such as corporations? George Cabot Lodge takes the above holistic approach when he argues that in order to deal with the realities of contemporary business, a manager must be willing "to confront manifold change openly and with a breadth of vision.... He must see his task as a general not a specialized one.... He is an integrator, a synthesizer, responsible for the whole and capable of perceiving the whole, within and without."[25]

I have suggested that wisdom is an essential virtue because it relates to the good of a whole, e.g., the good of an organization, and it is from a proper or improper conception of this good that virtues or vices in the organization flow. The classical source of the notion that wisdom is essential to all virtue is Plato's *Meno* (87d-89a). In this dialogue, Plato raises the question, what is virtue? After Meno offers some unsatisfactory answers and fails in his attempt to sabotage the discussion by arguing that inquiry is impossible, Socrates, himself, takes over. He develops an argument that shows that wisdom (*phronēsis*) is essential to all virtue and his argument is based on the premise, mentioned above, virtue is a good and, therefore, is always beneficial. Using an eliminative argument, he first lists plausible alternatives (things considered to be good or beneficial), viz., external goods (goods of the body and material goods) and internal goods. External goods are either beneficial or harmful depending upon whether or not they are guided by *phronēsis*, and similarly with internal goods. Both, as divorced from *phronēsis*, are eliminated by the regulative premise. In the course of this argument, he shows that traits conventionally associated with such virtues as courage and temperance cannot rightly be called by these names when the related conduct is not guided by *phronēsis*, for they just as readily lead to what is harmful as to what is beneficial.

If what I have said above is correct, it should be clear that an approach to the P2 problem of business ethics would benefit considerably from an analysis of values that have determined the character of American businesspeople. Such an analysis will reveal that each of the basic American business character types (the Protestant ethic, frontier ethic, robber baron ethic, viz., the traditional interrelated forms of our individualistic business tradition, and the organization man ethic, its modern antithesis) is still with us and, indeed, in many people they exist as conflicting elements of a complex life style. The above analysis would help the businessperson to understand the source of his or her own character and values as a businessperson.[26]

An analysis of American business values and character types will help us to understand the moral deficiencies of modern American business. This analysis is also necessary if we are to discover practical and effective ways of developing a business ethic that accords well with our moral sensibilities.[27] Business ethics, as a study, should attempt to formulate a practically possible business ethic which restores to American businesspeople the respect they believe is their due. Chapters 2 and 3 will analyze American business values and character models basically for the purpose of displaying their moral inadequacies and, therefore, understanding what must be changed if a Platonic type of solution is possible. However, in this connection, it is necessary to clarify the subtitle of the book, "Reflections from a Platonic Point of View." This subtitle applies primarily to Chapters 4 through 7. As I mentioned in the Preface, Chapters 4 and 5 present a Platonic critique of American business leadership from an ethical point of view, while Chapters 6 and 7 develop a Platonic type of business management theory that I believe is both defensible and viable. Although neither the style nor the substance of Chapters 2 and 3 purports to be Platonic, each provides the material (American business values and character models) that Chapters 4 and 5 criticize in a Platonic manner. Moreover, Chapter 6, in which I develop a Platonic type of ethical management, attempts to remedy the moral difficulties that are uncovered by my analysis of American business values in Chapters 2 and 3. Thus, these two chapters are necessary for both the subsequent negative and positive application of Platonic ethical and political theory to business ethics.

Although I would not argue that Plato engages in the type of historical analysis I provide in Chapters 2 and 3, he would emphasize the importance of reflecting on the influence of dominant values in a tradition on the character of people brought up in that tradition. This is the guiding idea behind the next two chapters.[28]

NOTES

1. Ethical egoism (the moral rightness or wrongness of person X's actions is determined solely by the good or bad consequences of these actions for X) and ethical altruism (the moral rightness of X's actions is determined solely by the good or bad consequences of these actions for others) are two other types of teleological moral theories. These positions are generally considered to be more objectionable than utilitarianism by philosophers who favor teleological moral theories.

2. The following questions can be asked of utilitarians: Should we try to maximize the average or total happiness of human beings? Should we emphasize the maximization of happiness or the minimization of suffering? Attempts to answer these questions would show that the utilitarian principle could not be the fundamental moral principle, for another principle(s) would be needed to resolve these problems.

3. Thus, Smart argues, "To refuse to break a generally beneficial rule in those cases in which it is not most beneficial to obey it seems irrational and to be a case of rule worship." J. J. C. Smart and Bernard Williams, *Utilitarianism for and against* (London: Cambridge University Press, 1973), p. 10.

4. The problem, however, is complex, for David Lyons argues that an adequate form of rule utilitarianism would yield the same conclusions as act utilitarianism, while Smart maintains that an adequate rule utilitarianism collapses into act utilitarianism (Smart and Williams, p. 10).

5. To give another example, Singer says, "Is it obvious, for example, that slavery, a system in which one group of people is held in subjection to the wishes and orders of another, does not and cannot produce a greater amount of happiness on the whole than any alternative system? It can be argued…that, provided that the number of slaves is kept relatively small, the benefits produced by the system…may be greater in amount and extent than the unhappiness produced by it." Marcus G. Singer, *Generalization in Ethics: An Essay in the Logic of Ethics with the Rudiments of a System of Moral Philosophy* (New York: Alfred A. Knoff, 1961), p. 195.

6. More familiar examples of deontological ethics are the moral commandments contained in the Ten Commandments and the Christian commandment to love one's neighbor. (The Ten Commandments, however, were never intended to constitute a complete ethical code.)

7. Kant has sometimes been accused of denying that the consequences of an action are relevant to its being right or wrong, but this is nonsense; by asking, what if everyone did that, one must clearly appeal to the consequences of a proposed action.

8. Kant seems to believe that such types of actions as telling the truth and keeping promises are unconditional duties which hold in all circumstances, but some philosophers believe that Kant has not applied his own categorical imperative correctly; if he did, they suggest, he would have admitted exceptions to rules (cf. Singer, pp. 228–233).

9. As Singer says, "What does it mean to treat every individual as an end in himself? Does it mean that a government has no right to conscript a man against his will and make him kill some fellow man in battle or be killed himself? Does it mean that in building a road or bridge we may not expropriate individuals who are attached to their ancestral homes" (Singer, p. 234)?

10. See, for example, G. E. M. Anscombe, "Modern Moral Philosophy," *Philosophy*, vol. 33 (1958): 1–19; Philippa Foot, *Virtues and Vices and Other Essays in Moral Philosophy* (Berkeley: University of California Press, 1978).

11. Alasdair MacIntyre, *After Virtue: A Study in Moral Virtue* (Notre Dame, Indiana: University of Notre Dame Press, 1981), p. 172. However, according to MacIntyre, there are "at least three very different conceptions of a virtue to confront: a virtue is a quality which enables an individual to discharge his or her social role (Homer); a virtue is a quality which enables an individual to move towards the achievement of the specifically human *telos*, whether natural or supernatural (Aristotle, the New Testament and Aquinas); a virtue is a quality which has utility in achieving earthly and heavenly success (Franklin)" (p. 173). MacIntyre believes that there is "a unitary core concept of the virtues" common to rival claims about virtue (p. 174). It is beyond the scope of this book to examine this issue properly. As the subtitle of the book suggests, I shall take a Platonic view

of virtue; this position fits the category in which MacIntyre places the Aristotelian and New Testament concept of virtue.

12. In the *Republic*, Polemarchus "inherits" the conventional morality of his father, Cephalus. He maintains that justice is doing good to friends and harm to enemies—in more familiar terms, an eye for an eye and a tooth for a tooth. Socrates finds no fault with doing good to anyone, but he objects to the view that a just person should intentionally harm an enemy who is evil. He argues that since justice is a virtue, a human excellence, it must be productive of what is beneficial (good) rather than harmful (*Republic* 335a–e). In the broadest sense, it should not only be productive of what is good for others, as if justice were merely another person's good, but also be beneficial to the agent. Thus, against Polemarchus's definition of justice, one might argue that not only is conduct based upon his view destructive of society, it is harmful to the human soul by nurturing the hateful, rather than loving, emotions. In the *Republic*, Socrates attempts to show that justice in his sense is basic to both the health of the individual and the city.

13. The fact that business emphasizes a rule-based, rather than a virtue-based, ethic is illustrated by the following remark. "On November 10, 1987, the *Wall Street Journal* reported the results of more than two hundred company codes of conduct. The most ignored item was personal character—it seemed not to matter." Clarence C. Walton, *The Moral Manager* (Cambridge, Mass.: Ballinger Pub. Co., 1988), p. 170.

14. For supporting evidence see Robbin Derry and Ronald M. Green, "Ethical Theory in Business Ethics: a Critical Assessment," *Journal of Business Ethics* (1989): 521–533. The following remarks are typical of the sentiments of business ethics theorists. With reference to moral reasoning in business, De George says, "The tools applicable in this endeavor are knowledge of ethical principles and mastering of the techniques of utilitarian and deontological moral argumentation." Richard T. De George, *Business Ethics* (New York: Macmillan, 1982), p. 69. With reference to action verses agent-based ethical theories, Velasquez says, "Sometimes moral principles also seem to be used to evaluate the moral worth of *persons* and *intentions*. We can safely ignore these uses, however, because the evaluations of actions seems to be more basic." Manuel G. Velasquez, *Business Ethics* (Englewood Cliffs, New Jersey: Prentice-Hall, 1982), p. 9 n. 15.

15. Peter F. Drucker, "Ethical Chic," *Forbes* (Sept. 14 1981): 160–173.

16. Edmund L. Pincoffs, *Quandaries and Virtues: Against Reductionism in Ethics* (Kansas: University Press of Kansas, 1986), p. 14.

17. Pincoffs, pp. 15–16.

18. For a discussion of this, see my article, "Plato on the Relation between Character Education and Rationality," *Southern Journal of Philosophy*, vol. 27, # 2 (Summer 1989): 239–254.

19. MacIntyre, p. 145.

20. If I were to approach business ethics in the standard fashion rather than in the way I do in this book (Platonic virtue ethics), it would have been necessary to discuss modern ethical theories and the criticisms of these theories in much more depth.

21. Tom L. Beauchamp and Norman E. Bowie, eds., *Ethical Theory and Business* (Englewood Cliffs, New Jersey: Prentice-Hall, 1979).

22. *Hare and Critics: Essays on Moral Thinking*, eds. Douglas Seanor and N. Fotion, with comments by R. M. Hare (Oxford: Clarendon Press, 1988), pp. 205–206. It should be noted that Hare's method of moral reasoning does not purport to yield true moral judgments.

23. I have criticized their positions in "The Value of *Endoxa* in Ethical Argument," *History of Philosophy Quarterly*, vol. 9, #2 (April 1992): 141–157.

24. Roger M. D'Aprix, *In Search of a Corporate Soul* (New York: Amacon, 1976).

25. George C. Lodge, "Business and the Changing Society," in *Issues in Business and Society*, eds. George A. Steiner and John F. Steiner, 2nd ed. (New York: Random House, 1977), p. 144.

26. MacIntyre says, "We are, whether we acknowledge it or not, what the past has made us and we cannot eradicate from ourselves, even in America, those parts of ourselves which are formed by our relationship to each formative stage in our history" (MacIntyre, p. 122). There is a good deal to be said for this position, although I think that one should emphasize the possibility of being able to change one's character. Therefore, one should also argue that understanding one's character entails understanding what has tended to form the type of character one possesses; such knowledge is, then, necessary if one wishes to determine what should be changed about one's character.

27. This project is useful in analyzing and evaluating the common pessimism about business ethics and helping us to find a way out of the deeper philosophical pessimism concerning the possibility of a moral organization (see Appendix I).

28. I have suggested that, in the *Republic*, materialistic values are seen to undermine character. Thus, Plato abolishes private property among his guardians—philosopher-kings and soldiers. He would, therefore, have been concerned about the negative moral effects of the frontiersman's and robber baron's materialistic and narrowly individualistic values. Thrasymachus, the model of the self-centered materialistic individualist in the *Republic*, is a central character because his ideal must be refuted if Plato's city is to be viable. But Plato is also concerned with the effect of every value on the character of a person. In the *Republic*, Homeric religious ideas (ideas about the gods and the afterlife that molded ancient Greek religion) are censored because of their negative effect on character. Plato would, therefore, have been concerned about the effect of the Protestant ethic (Calvinistic values) on the character of American businesspeople.

CHAPTER II

AMERICAN BUSINESS VALUES PART I
PREDEPRESSION AMERICAN BUSINESS VALUES

Predepression American business values can be characterized as materialistic individualism. The tendency toward business amorality, and even immorality, deepens as this value system develops from the Protestant to the frontier and, finally, the robber baron ethic. These three forms of what might be called the traditional American business value system are different but interrelated.

1. The Protestant Ethic and Its Moral Implications

According to the noted authority on Puritanism, Perry Miller, the Puritan philosophy of life was neither conducive to democracy nor to religious freedom. "Puritanism appears, from the sacred and economic point of view, to have been a philosophy of social stratification, placing the command in the hands of the properly qualified and demanding implicit obedience from the uneducated."[1] These "expounders of holy writ were to be the mentors of farmers and merchants."[2] Less than sympathetic interpreters of Puritanism, e.g., Vernon Parrington, believe that the phrase "Puritan open-mindedness" is an oxymoron. "Academic thinkers and schoolmen, men whom the free spaces of thought frightened and who felt safe only behind secure fences, theologians like John Cotton and his fellows, made a virtue of necessity and fell to declaiming on the excellences of those chains wherewith they were bound."[3] More sympathetic interpreters, such as Miller, take issue with this view. Miller argues that Puritan leaders were humanists in the sense of being students of classical literature, although he admits that their theology prevented a proper appreciation of it. "It is enough to say here that study of the arts and sciences and of good literature was among the purposes of education in New England as well as the learning of theology."[4] The object of such humanistic education was the development of one's reason. Nonetheless, Miller admits that "there was almost always an element of narrowness, harshness, and literal-mindedness associated with Puritanism."[5]

Puritanism, in its early years, was not favorable to the development of business. Many Puritans believed in "government regulation of business, the fixing of just prices, and the curtailing of individual profits in the interests of the welfare of the whole."[6] However, a conflict developed between the Presbyterian oligarchy and the Puritan merchants. Early Puritan leaders, such as John Cotton, failed to see the implicit inconsistency in Puritan values; they did not see the conflict between a medieval antibusiness ethic and their doctrine of a calling which was consistent with a business ethic that emphasized industry. Max Weber coined the term "the Protestant ethic" for Calvinist views that underlie Puritan business values. As merchants grew strong enough to assert their independence of early clerical restraints, the church had to respect the businessman's pursuits. What is the source of the Protestant ethic, and what are its traits (insofar as they are related to business)? According to Luther, all legitimate work is sacred. This provides the basis of what Weber refers to as Martin Luther's conception of a calling, i.e., a person's performance of his duties in worldly affairs is required by God as a religious obligation.[7] But the Puritans were Calvinists. John Calvin relates this doctrine to his belief in the moral depravity of human nature and the predestination of an elect few. Absorption in worldly affairs is essential because it diverts attention from doubts about personal salvation, and in accomplishing good works through one's calling (a Christian's most important duty), one should improve one's station in life as an assurance of being one of God's elect.[8] The ethic of dutiful absorption in work leads to a list of "virtues," which together, has been called the Protestant ethic. Although such traits as orderliness, cleanliness, chastity, and moderation were emphasized, those essential to business were industry, frugality, thrift, sobriety, and austerity. Cotton Mather, a famous (religious) Puritan spokesman of these virtues, argues that no one could get into heaven without a settled business. Benjamin Franklin, the most famous secular expounder of these virtues, maintains that they were essential to gaining wealth. Generally, Puritans defended business success and its implied materialism, not in itself, but rather as a sign of one's virtues; by means of these virtues, material success is achieved and assurance of being one of God's elect is reinforced.[9] Finally, it is argued that the most successful Puritans, being the most virtuous, are the stewards or the true guardians of the wealth (for the glory of God); they are God's trustees "of the goods which have come to them through God's grace."[10]

Although this ethic is not without its admirable aspects, some of its consequences are ethically unpalatable. A particularly odious effect of the Protestant ethic is that it encourages disdain for the poor or less privileged. It is, therefore, productive of an antihumanistic value system. Just as wealth, on this view, is a sign of virtue, poverty is considered a sign of vice, e.g., laziness, lack of drive and perseverance, inability to manage money properly, too frivolous an attitude toward business, and the like.[11] Obvious consequences of this attitude are neglect of morally necessary social legislation, social condemnation of the more unfortunate, and a general neglect of the finer (moral) feelings related to caring, concern, and sympathy for others. The narrowness of this ethic can hardly be productive of a properly moral standpoint; indeed, it is possible to root some of the legitimate moral criticisms of business in this attitude.

R. H. Tawney develops the above moral criticism of the Protestant ethic. He argues that in America, as well as England and elsewhere, Calvinism, which began as "the very soul of authoritarian regimentation," changed into a vehicle for an almost utilitarian individualism.[12] According to Tawney, The Puritan viewed the world as "a forbidding and frost-bound wilderness," one in which "he must take his way, alone."[13] Thus, he argues, "The moral self-sufficiency of the Puritan nerved his will, but it corroded his sense of social solidarity."[14] Tawney sees this individualism as the precursor of a form found among the captains of industry. Puritan individualism, based upon what Tawney calls "a private transaction between himself and his maker," helped to develop an ethic "in which the traditional scheme of Christian virtues [e.g., compassion] was almost exactly reversed, and which, since he was above all practical, he carried as a dynamic into the routine of business and political life."[15] The resulting inhumane ethic, which characterized "middle and commercial classes who were the citadel of the Puritan spirit," is described as follows.

> Convinced that character is all and circumstances nothing, he
> sees in the poverty of those who fall by the way, not a misfor-
> tune to be pitied and relieved, but a moral failing to be con-
> demned, and in riches, not an object of suspicion...but the
> blessing which rewards the triumph of energy and will.[16]

Tawney develops this theme in a chapter entitled "The New Medicine for
Poverty."[17] Such passages as the following reinforce the above quotation.

> That the greatest of evils is idleness, that the poor are the
> victims, not of circumstances, but of their own 'idle, irregular
> and wicked courses,' that the truest charity is not to enervate
> them by relief, but so to reform their characters that relief may
> be unnecessary—such doctrines turned severity from a sin into
> a duty, and froze the impulse of natural pity with the assurance
> that, if indulged, it would perpetuate the suffering which it
> sought to allay.[18]

Tawney suggests another major difficulty with the Protestant ethic. He
maintains that this ethic demands that "there must be no idle leisure,"[19] and
generally, emphasizes economic values. But, he argues, economic values must be
balanced against noneconomic values. An overemphasis on economic values by the
later Puritans undercuts more liberal ones. In his conclusion, Tawney argues against
an overemphasis on such values.

> But it cannot itself be merely economic, since the comparative
> importance of economic and of other interests—the sacrifice, for
> example, of material goods worth incurring in order to extend
> leisure, or develop education, or humanize toil—is precisely the
> point on which it is needed to throw light. It must be based on
> some conception of the requirements of human nature as a
> whole.[20]

Miller, we saw, who argues against the position that the Puritan value system
is fundamentally opposed to cultural and liberal arts pursuits, nonetheless seems to
be more willing to agree that this view applies to the ethic of the Puritan merchant
of the second half of the 17th century. In discussing the Protestant ethic he says,
"Merchants, farmers, and shipbuilders increased 'cent per cent,' and the consequence appeared to be a decay of godliness, class struggles, extravagant dress and

contempt for learning."[21] The Protestant ethic of industry was, itself, undermining the earlier Puritan beliefs. "The more diligently the people applied themselves...the more they produced a decay of religion and a corruption of morals."[22]

The Protestant ethic, as interpreted above, unduly narrows the individualism of the American businessperson. Cultural and liberal arts pursuits, on this view, tend to be seen as decadent. Individualism, in the above sense, is a truncated type of individualism. It should be compared with the more defensible form developed, for example, by Henry David Thoreau, in *Walden*. Individualism and personal freedom begin in temperance, which frees one's mind from the tyranny of appetites and those emotions which cause the mind to rationalize (in the pejorative sense) one's beliefs. In their highest form, they entail the development of the mind, wisdom, so that not only is one free to act on one's beliefs, one is not tyrannized by ignorance.

The truncated individualism of the Protestant ethic, which frees the mind from the tyranny of appetites only to enslave it to ignorance, is developed by Ralph Barton Perry. Perry calls the Puritan a "moral athlete" for he trains himself ruthlessly to suppress the appetites. This attitude entails what he calls "rigorism." It involves an overconcern with, and overattention to, the appetites as the enemy, rather than a desire to find a proper place for them. The result is an overemphasis on will and an underemphasis on thinking. Perry says that, according to the Puritan, "It may be difficult to *do* what one ought to do; but to *discover* what one ought to do is comparatively easy."[23] He correctly maintains that it is impossible to be truly virtuous with such a view, and moral difficulties which require judgment rather than a strong will remain unresolved. Morality requires a balanced, rather than an inflexible, mind.

Clarence C. Walton admires the modern executive who exhibits the temperance entailed by the Protestant ethic.

> The temperate executive is preferred over the intemperate one, and for one very good reason: overindulgence is bad ethics and bad business. Its manifestations are the spendthrift, the free-loader, and the hedonist. Its opposites are the thrift ethic, the work ethic, and the long-term ethic [that is, the Protestant ethic].[24]

But in developing this point, Walton allies temperance with a statesmanlike wisdom. "For managers, temperance means careful budgeting of all resources—financial, physical, and human—in order to make the organization continually viable in serving human needs."[25] We saw, however, that, according to Perry, statesmanlike wisdom is not to be found in Puritan morality.

2. The Frontier Ethic and Its Moral Implications

The opening up of the frontier reinforced the individualism (self-reliance), and intensified the materialism, of the Protestant ethic. It also, probably, helped to separate this value system from its religious emphasis as well as its antidemocratic leanings, viz., it bred a concern for freedom and equality. The character of Americans changed as they moved into the frontier. They became more absorbed in business and profits than in religion and salvation. The frontier reinforced the importance of practical success and nurtured the traits of coarseness and strength, animal cunning (having smarts), being able to find the expedient way to master practical problems (yankee know how or can do), boundless and nervous energy (being dynamic), and an insatiable love of liberty. These traits are readily recognizable as those traditionally admired by the American businessperson. Thus, for example, Matthew Josephson sees in the character of the robber barons, the traits Frederick Jackson Turner attributes to the frontiersman.[26]

Turner's Frontier Thesis is the seminal work on the importance of the frontier in American history. In his paper, "The Significance of the Frontier in American History," he summarizes the traits that comprise, what I have called, the frontier ethic.

> That coarseness and strength combined with acuteness and inquisitiveness; that practical, insensitive turn of mind, quick to find expedients; that masterful grasp of material things, lacking in the artistic but powerful to effect great ends; that restless, nervous energy; that dominant individualism; working for good and for evil, and withal that buoyancy and exuberance which comes from freedom.[27]

Commenting on the coarseness and narrow practicality of the frontier mentality James T. Adams says, "The learned and gentle were left behind, and rawness and lack of culture were increased."[28] Thus, the twin evils of the Protestant ethic with respect to business, the development among the later Puritan merchants of a cultural philistinism due to an overemphasis on wealth and their inhumane attitude toward the unfortunate, were reinforced. Adams suggests, "Just as American Puritanism had become intolerantly narrow, so was the life of the frontier; and thus two of the strongest influences in our life, religion and the frontier, made in our formative periods for a limited and intolerant spiritual life."[29]

Generally, the frontier ethic, according to Turner, nurtured a basically antisocial and strongly selfish individualism, and it was in this context that the Protestant ethic evolved. Turner associates the lack of civic spirit and business honor (morality), not to mention such evils as the spoils system, inflated paper currency and wildcat banking, with this frontier spirit. He says,

> But the democracy born of free land, strong in selfishness and individualism, intolerant of administrative experience and education, and pressing individual liberty beyond its proper bounds, has its dangers as well as its benefits. Individualism in America has allowed a laxity in regard to governmental affairs which has rendered possible the spoils system and all the manifest evils that follow from the lack of a highly developed civic spirit. In this connection may be noted also the influence of frontier conditions in permitting lax business honor, inflated paper currency and wildcat banking.[30]

Alexis de Tocqueville, probably the greatest of the commentators on American culture, also brought the latent moral difficulties of this ethic to the surface by showing that individualism overemphasizes self-reliance; it tends to draw a person too much into himself, severing himself, his friends, and his family from the community and from one's fellow human beings. Such people often view themselves as standing alone and are apt, often unrealistically, to view their destiny as totally in their own hands.[31] He distinguishes selfishness from individualism, arguing that selfishness entails an

exaggerated love of self, which leads a man to connect everything with himself and to prefer himself to everything in the
world.... Selfishness originates in blind instinct; individualism
proceeds from erroneous judgment more than from depraved
feelings; it originates as much in deficiencies of mind as in
perversity of heart.[32]

Tocqueville's comment about individualism is worth considering. It suggests
the importance of drawing on the insights of a Socratic ethic, one which
emphasizes the fact that evil originates in ignorance, in morally evaluating
traditional American business values. In morally evaluating the ethic of individualism, Tocqueville agrees with Turner that this value system tends to be morally
inadequate, sapping a person of the "virtues of the public life." Thus, Tocqueville
suggests, individualism "is at length absorbed in downright selfishness," rather than
escaping from its evils.[33]

It would be misleading if I were to leave this section without apprising the
reader of the fact that, although Turner's thesis was one of the most influential
positions in American history, it is not without its critics. But before discussing
this, it is necessary to summarize Turner's paper, "The Significance of the Frontier
in American History." Briefly, in this paper, he emphasizes expansion in
distinguishing Americans from Europeans. American cultural patterns changed as
Americans moved to new frontiers and attempted to adapt to the primitive
economic and political conditions of these frontier environments. Turner maintains
that the American character was formed by frontier experiences—"the crucible of
the frontier." Sparse population and abundant land provided greater opportunities
than existed in the more populated areas of the country. Supported by plentiful land
and resources, the frontier American developed an intensified concern for material
prosperity, but his individualism and belief in equality of opportunity also promoted
a faith in democracy. The pioneers' relative isolation helped them to be innovative
and creative, and their willingness to consider new opportunities developed in them
a habit of mobility. But their lifestyle undermined a respect for abstract thinking
and artistic creativity. Although this lack of respect for such activities is not unique
to Americans, Turner argues that it existed in Americans in an intensified form
because of frontier experiences.

Turner was more tentative about his thesis than his followers; indeed, they tended to be quite dogmatic. They maintained the highly debatable position that the frontier was the only force which molded the American character rather than the more defensible position that it was only one important force. On the opposite side were the more extreme critics of Turner's thesis who argued that the frontier was not even a major force in creating an American character. Other critics rejected specific aspects of his thesis—for example, his safety-valve theory, the view that democracy originated in the West rather than in Europe, and that the frontier produced individualistic rather than cooperative conduct. The thesis was severely criticized from the Depression to the late 1940's, but much of this criticism, and subsequent criticism, need not detain us, for much of it is irrelevant to my limited purpose in this section. It is sufficient to admit, for our purposes, that the frontier experiences did help to mold a pre-civil war character that exhibited, at least, many of the traits Turner attributes to the frontiersman—traits which play a substantial role in understanding the predepression American business character. However, this limited position, as suggested above, has been attacked by some of Turner's critics. These objections, as Harry C. Allen shows, can be satisfactorily countered.

Allen argues that Turner and his supporters may have overemphasized the degree of self-reliance and individualism developed by frontier experiences. But Turner never denied, what some critics emphasize, that the frontier necessitated mutual assistance. He argues, however, that to compare such necessary cooperation among frontiersmen with the degree of mutual dependence necessary in "more settled areas" is not reasonable and demonstrates a lack of a sense of proportion. Compared, he thinks, "to a closed society like that of many countries in Europe, we can still agree that, at least up to the Civil War, the American frontier was a breeding ground for self-reliance and individualism."[34] He argues further,

> Broad generalizations about whole societies are always difficult
> and seldom absolutely true, but it is not really possible to doubt
> the deep and lasting influence of the frontier upon the history
> of the United States, nor to question that it directly contributed
> to the formation of many of the most pronounced characteristics
> of the American people...[for example, American optimism and
> idealism]. But they needed more than that to conquer and

subdue a continental domain of three million square miles. They
needed great ingenuity and prodigious energy.[35]

3. The Robber Baron Ethic and Its Moral Implications

The evils of the above ethic are seen, almost in caricature, in the activities of the
robber barons, the captains of industry and finance who dominated the American
scene in the latter half of the 19th century and at the turn of the 20th. From Matthew
Josephson, who coined the term "robber baron," to contemporaries such as Robert
Heilbroner, the robber barons' excesses, resulting from their value system, have
been roundly condemned. Concerning their materialism, Josephson maintains, "to
organize and exploit the resources of a nation upon a gigantic scale,…and to do
this only in the name of uncontrolled appetite for private profit—here surely is the
great inherent contradiction whence so much disaster, outrage and misery has
flowed."[36] Their extreme concern for materialistic values was matched by an, at
least, equally extreme form of individualism. Heilbroner speaks of them as bold,
aggressive, acquisitive, competitors who manipulated both consumers and
shareholders, and, in cutthroat competitive fashion, attempted to undercut all
competition.[37] The narrow self-interest of the early industrial giants is captured in
the following remarks by Thomas C. Cochran and William Miller.

> In place of the old canons, they imposed the rule of the jungle
> upon a willing people who worshipped at the altar of 'progress.'
> Remorselessly they exploited precious resources, stripped
> incomparable forests, leaving gaping holes in mountain sides to
> mark exhausted mines, dotting with abandoned derricks oil
> fields drained of petroleum and natural gas. In reckless haste,
> they constructed railroads through the wilderness, and immense
> factories to supply the needs of millions yet unborn. They
> promoted many similar projects simply to mulct a nation of
> speculators for the private benefit of the 'fittest.'[38]

Concerning their ethics, Stewart Holbrook, who calls them "moguls," says,

> The best of them made 'deals,' purchased immunity, and did
> other things which in 1860, or 1880, or even 1900, were
> considered not more than 'smart' by their fellow Americans, but

which today would give pause to the most conscientiously dishonest promoter. The rules have a way of changing every decade or so.... Indeed, under present-day rules, almost every man in this book would face a good hundred years in prison.[39]

To their admirers, however, and there have been many, their combined virtues provide the model for the ideal businessman. To them, the robber barons were "nature's noblemen," modern nobility being equated with success in business. They were models of the self-made man.[40] As Holbrook suggests, the robber barons "were men of devout and adamantine individualism" who, driven by "an overpowering sense of acquisitiveness," dealt with the world as it is rather than as it ought to be.[41] A number of robber barons, e.g., John D. Rockefeller, Daniel Drew, and Andrew Carnegie, were influenced by the Protestant ethic,[42] but these virtues, which thrived in the context of small business operations, were no longer sufficient for the successful businessperson in a large industrial or financial firm. Reflecting on the virtues of the robber barons emphasized by their defenders, one can readily see the dominant influence of the frontier ethic. Their admirers pointed to the importance of shrewdness, nerve (courage), self-confidence, initiative, tremendous energy (drive), and the will to win. These traits were considered to be essential if one were to be a successful competitor in the world of big business. It is obvious that these virtues are much admired by today's businesspeople. Their detractors, on the other hand, presented a different picture of the robber barons' so-called virtues. To Thorstein Veblen, one of the most famous critics of the robber barons, their activities were not only pecuniary, but predatory as well. They exhibited the traits of "shrewd" traders and "unscrupulous" managers. "Chicanery," rather than honesty and good will, was basic to the character of these captains of industry and finance.[43]

The robber barons argued, as the Puritan leaders did, that the wealthy (themselves) are the natural leaders—the Puritan ideal of stewardship.[44] But their narrow materialistic value system left them with little understanding of culture or, for that matter, anything other than making money. Many of the robber barons were models of philistinism. According to James T. Adams, they had no time or inclination for thinking in areas outside of industry and finance.[45] Their religion was at the intellectual level of superstition or was seen, as in the case of James J.

Hill, as having practical advantages. The "cultural" activity of many of the robber barons was dominated by conspicuous consumption; they indulged themselves in buying art, but many of them were noted for their bad taste. Nonetheless, from 1900–1929 a number of articulate admirers of their style became the self-professed mouthpieces of their ethic for a very large segment of the American public.[46] For example, George Lorimer, of the old Saturday Evening Post, argued for the subordination of the virtues of the gentleman—the virtues of culture and the liberal arts—to those of material success.[47] One result, therefore, of the traditional American business ethic is a concerted devaluation of the liberal arts.[48] Milton Friedman, in arguing against the modern conception of corporate social responsibility, suggests the dangers of placing social power in the hands of businesspeople whose focus is the market rather than values.[49] The pursuit of wealth—which the robber barons argued ennobles people by developing their virtues, enriches society by creating opportunities for others, and provides goods and services that society needs—is not a school for the development of moral character. It nurtures a narrow self-interest and creates devastation for those who are not the "winners."

Two basic moral props were used by the robber barons and their supporters to defend their activities, viz., the idea of universal opportunities for advancement and the theory of Social Darwinism. The former idea was used to root all failure, and its resultant misery, in defects of character and will. The mass of Americans who did not make it were considered losers who had lost their courage and parasitically depended on those who still possessed the will to win. The gap between the millionaire and the proletariat was, then, defended on the basis of the robber barons' virtues which allowed them to grasp the opportunities that existed. After all, it was argued, they were the driving force behind material progress and created opportunities for others. They should, therefore, be entitled to the lion's share of the wealth; indeed, if government does not hinder them, this is exactly what they will get. In essence, this position attempted to provide more support for the Puritan view which equated wealth with virtue and poverty with vice.[50] But the premise of this position, the universal opportunities for advancement in this country, has been shown to be a myth by a number of studies.[51] This myth merely reinforced the amorality, if not immorality, and the downright callousness of traditional American business.

Their other basic moral defense, Social Darwinism,[52] was developed by Herbert Spencer. According to Spencer, ruthless competition among individuals (and races), uncontrolled individualism, and the elimination of the weak and unfit are the best guarantees of moral and social as well as material progress. Those who survive the dog-eat-dog competition are the fittest or the best, and it is these people who create progress. Spencer was consistent in applying his theory. He repudiated aid to the poor, rejected state supported education, sanitary supervision, regulation of housing, and state protection of people from medical fakes. Spencer's theory received the wholehearted endorsement of the captains of industry and finance. Carnegie, Rockefeller, and Hill, for example, were fond of quoting Spencer and were devout admirers of his theory. Sidney Fine says,

> That part of Spencer's thought that dealt with the struggle for existence, the survival of the fittest as the result of natural selection, and the inevitability of progress was readily adaptable to the pattern of American economic life and to the needs of the businessman. It took no great imagination to see that Spencer offered a rationale for the business triumphs of the industrial leaders and for opposition to all proposals of state intervention on behalf of the unsuccessful.[53]

Thus, like laissez-faire theory, the narrow self-interest motivation of business is defended by the "moral" result. Although Adam Smith's theory, as applied to small business, has great merit, the theory of Social Darwinism has no merit whatsoever.[54] The fittest are not necessarily the ethically best, and evolution cannot be equated with moral and social progress. Darwin's phrase "the survival of the fittest" is tautologous—the survivors survive.

4. An Interlude—The Medici

During the 15th century in Florence, Italy, four members of the Medici family —Giovanni, Cosimo, Piero, and Lorenzo—wielded great power and influence. Giovanni, Cosimo, and Piero were immensely successful businessmen, but their values are in stark contrast to those of the robber barons and, in many ways, predepression American business values in general. During this period of the

Renaissance, they exemplified the Renaissance man. It may, therefore, be helpful briefly to consider their values, values which the reader will note are considerably broader than those of the traditional American businessperson. The contrast between the values of the Medici and traditional American businesspeople is especially helpful in countering the view that business must be predicated upon narrow self-interest and, generally, a narrow materialistic view of values. The moral example that their lives provide should give pause to anyone who thinks that business should be oriented toward purely economic values rather than those broad-based values that characterize wisdom and truly produce the greatest good for the greatest number. This later view, I shall argue, is related to a Platonic conception of business statesmanship.

The Medici were already successful bankers by the time the first great Medici, Giovanni di Bicci de' Medici, was the head of the family. Giovanni was a distinguished financier, and at his death he left an immense fortune to his two sons, Cosimo and Lorenzo.[55] Col. G. F. Young says, "He died deservingly esteemed by his countrymen, beloved by the humbler classes of the people, who had so often found in him a defender and whose welfare he had consistently promoted, remembered with gratitude by all who, struggling to rise in some branch of art, had never failed to receive from him a helping hand."[56]

The above statement about the father of the Medici sets the values for this family through Lorenzo the Magnificent. By the time Cosimo de' Medici was the head of the family, the Medicis had amassed enormous wealth, "owning banks in as many as sixteen capital cities in Europe."[57] However, their values were fundamentally humane and liberal; wealth was for the purpose of the greater good of their city rather than for private gain. This value system should be contrasted with traditional American business predepression values.

Cosimo de' Medici was magnanimous and he showed concern for the people whom he governed. He both relieved the crushing tax burden on the poor and developed Florentine markets, and therefore their wealth, by prudent guidance of foreign affairs so as to make wars less frequent. Although he was a most successful businessman and a "financier of the first rank,"[58] he was also a strong supporter of humanism and one of history's great patrons of the arts. As Edward Gibbon says, "His riches were dedicated to the service of mankind,"[59] i.e., to the advancement of learning and the arts, and the material betterment of his fellow citizens.

In no way, then, did Cosimo's upbringing as a merchant, or for that matter the upbringing of Giovanni, conflict with the humanistic influences of the time.[60] One of Cosimo's lifetime ambitions was to create an academy of Platonic studies. Although a merchant, he was instructed in the classics and throughout his life he retained a genuine interest in their advancement.[61] He supported efforts to unearth classical manuscripts, founded libraries to house such books, and supported all of the outstanding humanists of the age. As a patron of the arts, he supported architects, sculptors, and painters.

Although Piero de' Medici was not as illustrious as his father Cosimo and certainly not as famous as his son Lorenzo (Piero ruled Florence for only five years), he inherited the business and humanistic concerns of his father. Ferdinand Schevill maintains that "Under his guidance, which, again like his father's, was a mixture of boldness and caution, its [the Medici bank] fortunes...reached the highest level they ever attained."[62] Yet, like his father, he supported humanistic scholarship, libraries (Schevill calls him an "ardent bibliophile"[63]), and the arts.

As admirable as Giovanni, Cosimo, and Piero were, it was Lorenzo the Magnificent who perfected the virtues of the Medici family. According to Young, he was called magnificent "because of his extraordinary abilities, his great liberality, his lavish expenditure of his wealth for the public benefit, and the general magnificence of his life in which Florence participated."[64] He excelled as a statesman, classical scholar, poet, and writer. Moreover, he advanced learning and the arts more than any other Medici. Under his direction, Florence became "the intellectual and artistic capital of Europe."[65] It may be argued that in no other city, with the exception of Athens, did intellectual and artistic values flourish more than they did under the tutelage of Lorenzo.

Although Lorenzo was arguably, more than any other Medici, the model Renaissance man, it is unclear what his place in my scenario should be. By all accounts, he was not the businessman that his predecessors had been. Francesco Guicciardini argues that "he knew little and cared less about business" and, therefore, the Medici bank suffered because its affairs were, at times, managed by men of "little ability."[66] "On several occasions," says Guicciardini, "his affairs were in such disorder that he was on the verge of bankruptcy, and was forced to avail himself of his friend's money or the public funds."[67] Schevill attributes the problems that Lorenzo had with the Medici bank to "an impatience he developed with the dull details of business."[68] According to Schevill, Lorenzo also had "insufficient commercial training."[69] Therefore, although he is arguably "the finest flowering to which the family [the Medici] attained,"[70] some of his character traits were apparently in conflict with the virtues of a successful businessperson.

Possibly, however, we are taking a too narrow view of the virtues related to business leadership. If a business leader should concern himself or herself with the profitability of a firm and the benefits that accrue to the stakeholders, it may be argued that although Lorenzo may have neglected the family's monetary interests, he did not neglect the economic interests of the Florentine people, and he satisfied their desires as "stakeholders." Therefore, what may be viewed as a lack of virtue with respect to narrow business concerns, may not be so if we consider managerial leadership in its broadest terms.

Guicciardini, whom we have seen had little respect for Lorenzo's business abilities, nonetheless mentions the material prosperity of Florence and the development of the trades during Lorenzo's rule.[71] Schevill, who is equally critical of Lorenzo's management of his business affairs, says that under his humane rule, "Florence enjoyed a better civil order and a greater security of life and goods than any other community of the peninsula."[72] Clearly, then, Lorenzo was an exemplary statesman. Indeed, Lorenzo exhibited abilities that we shall see, in subsequent chapters, are central to Platonic statesmanship. He, like other members of his family, had the statesmanlike ability to get people, who would ordinarily be antagonistic to one another, to work harmoniously together. Moreover, he had the ability to create friends out of political enemies, and generally to maintain the peace in circumstances which could easily have erupted into war.[73]

5. Traditional American Business Values and Their Institutional Support

Traditional American business values, which I have characterized as generally individualistic and materialistic, were reinforced by religious, economic, and political systems which provided their theoretical justification. I shall limit myself to a very brief discussion of the pertinent theories.

Protestantism is more individualistic than Catholicism, and the antimaterialistic stance of Medieval Catholicism gave way, as we saw, to Calvinistic support for business.[74] Laissez-faire theory, from an economics standpoint, and Jeffersonian democracy, from a political standpoint, both provided a defense for traditional American business values.

American individualism—with its concern for self-reliance, personal freedom, and equality of opportunity—was supported by the doctrine that the government that governs least governs best. Dividing power rather than enlarging it was seen as the best safeguard for our freedoms. In government, our founding fathers argued for the separation of powers and the division of powers among federal, state, and local governments. James Madison, in *Federalist #10*, attempts to defend representative republic, rather than direct democracy, on the grounds that it could better control the tyranny of the majority. Democracy, in the broad sense, is itself an expression of the deep suspicion of political power.

Thomas Jefferson valued personal freedom in the sense that each person has the right to live his or her own life, and develop himself, in accordance with (hopefully) reflective values. His basic concern, on first seeing the Constitution, was that it contained no explicit safeguards for people's rights. People in a free society have the right to pursue happiness in their own way, that is, in accordance with their diverse personalities.

In Adam Smith's version of a free economy, power, again, is divided up into relatively small pieces because small businesses would dominate, rather than monopolies or oligopolies. Each merchant is free to act as he wishes; in a business context, he will act out of self-interest—aim toward profit and away from loss. Competition, or supply and demand, would create equity among the economic variables, viz., prices, profits, wages, and the quantity and quality of goods. Greater inequities would result from government control of business. Laissez-faire helps to make economic opportunity and self-determination possible in the context of Jeffersonian democracy which, itself, supports self-determination and opportunity in the broad sense of the term.

Both laissez-faire theory and American political theory have a materialistic base. For laissez-faire theory, all of the economic variables are guided by competition, to a just and socially fruitful end. All merchants have to do is act out of self-interest, i.e., aim toward profit and away from loss. Laissez-faire, then, purports to be a self-regulating system motivated by self-interested individuals. Our traditional political system supports the view that government exists to protect life and property, i.e., the Lockean position. Material values are of central importance and without government, our lives and property are too insecure.

NOTES

1. Perry Miller and Thomas H. Johnson, *The Puritans*, vol. 1, rev. ed. (New York: Harper and Row, 1963), p. 19.

2. Miller and Johnson, p. 19.

3. Vernon L. Parrington, *Main Currents in American Thought*, vols. one, two, and three (New York: Harcourt, Brace and Co., 1927), p. 12. James Truslow Adams [*The Epic of America* (New York: Garden City Books, 1933)] presents an equally unflattering picture of Puritan intellectuality. "Throughout its first century and more, the leaders in New England steadily declined in humane culture.... Lack of intercourse with others tended to emphasize the New Englander's deep-rooted belief in his own superiority as the chosen vessel of God for the regeneration of the world.... The intellectual life that remained came to be pedantic and narrow rather than humane and broad, with both conscience and thrift operating against much that is valuable in social life and the arts" (p. 44; cf. p. 32).

4. Miller and Johnson, p. 20. Also see, Samuel Eliot Morison, *The Intellectual Life of Colonial New England* (New York: New York University Press, 1956).

5. Miller and Johnson, p. 59.

6. Miller and Johnson, p. 5.

7. Max Weber, *The Protestant Ethic and the Spirit of Capitalism*, trans. Talcott Parsons (New York: Charles Scribner's Sons, 1958), p. 80.

8. Weber, pp. 111–112, 115. Tawney, reflecting on the Calvinist businessperson's view of a calling, says that "from this reiterated insistence on secular obligations

as imposed by the divine will, it follows that...the conscientious discharge of the duties of business, is among the loftiest of religious and moral virtues." R. H. Tawney, *Religion and the Rise of Capitalism* (Gloucester, Mass.: Peter Smith, 1926), p. 240. "Success in business," he argues, "is in itself almost a sign of spiritual grace, for it is proof that a man has labored faithfully in his vocation, and that 'God has blessed his trade'" (p. 246).

9. Weber, pp. 162–163.

10. Weber, pp. 170; cf. p. 162.

11. Weber, for example, p. 122.

12. Tawney, p. 227.

13. Tawney, p. 228.

14. Tawney, p. 229.

15. Tawney, pp. 229–230.

16. Tawney, p. 230. James Oliver Robertson [*America's Business* (New York: Hill and Wang, 1985)] argues that the rise of slavery in America occurred when attitudes justifying forced labor of the poor in England were prevalent. He maintains that "The spread of such attitudes may well have accompanied the spread of the 'Protestant work ethic' in the years after the collapse of the Puritan commonwealth in England" (p. 38). Americans, he suggests, were imitating their English counterparts; Africans were called "a brutish people." "They, like servants and the poor, were 'shiftless, irresponsible, unfaithful, ungrateful, dishonest; they got drunk whenever possible; they did not work hard enough or regularly enough'" (p. 38). Thus, a defense of slavery for the profit of the owners was based upon a justification implicit in the Protestant ethic—poverty is the sign of vice.

17. Tawney, pp. 253–273.

18. Tawney, p. 266.

19. Tawney, p. 242.

20. Tawney, pp. 283–284. Walton comments on the modern businessperson's narrow perspective on values. He suggests that overemphasis on the importance of business in society creates a truncated view of our social responsibilities and our obligations in general. One consequence of this is the setting up of a double standard for business and for the rest of society. Business success is all important,

and the end justifies the means. Walton, *The Moral Manager* (Cambridge, Mass.: Ballinger Pub. Co., 1988), pp. 19–20.

21. Perry Miller, *The New England Mind: from Colony to Province* (Cambridge, Mass.: Harvard University Press, 1962), p. 40.

22. Miller, p. 51.

23. Ralph Barton Perry, "The Moral Athlete" in George M. Waller *Puritanism in Early America* (Boston: D.C. Heath and Co., 1950), p. 106.

24. Walton, p. 180.

25. Walton, p. 180.

26. Matthew Josephson, *The Robber Barons: The Great American Capitalists* (New York: Harcourt Brace and Co., 1934), pp. 20–23.

27. Frederick Jackson Turner, *The Significance of the Frontier in American History* (Ann Arbor: University Microfilms Inc., 1966), pp. 226–227.

28. Adams, p. 94.

29. Adams, p. 96. Concerning the influence of narrow practicality on the nurturing of anti-intellectualism and an "intolerant spiritual life," Richard Hofstadter [*Anti-Intellectualism in American Life* (New York: Alfred A. Knopf, 1964)] says, "The anti-intellectualism of businessmen...interpreted...broadly as a suspicion of intellect itself,...is part of the extensive American devotion to practicality and direct experience which ramifies through almost every area of American life.... Practical vigor is a virtue; what has been spiritually crippling in our history is the tendency to make a mystique of practicality" (pp. 236–237).

30. Turner, p. 223.

31. Alexis de Tocqueville, *Democracy in America*, vol. II (New York: Vintage Books, 1956), pp. 105–106.

32. Tocqueville, p. 104.

33. Tocqueville, p. 104.

34. H. C. Allen, "F. J. Turner and the Frontier in American History," reprinted in *The Frontier Thesis: Valid Interpretation of American History?* ed. Ray Allen Billington (New York: Holt, Rinehart and Winston, 1966), p. 114. Dale Van Every [*Forth to the Wilderness: The First American Frontier* (New York: William Morrow and Co., 1961)] argues that early in the frontier experience, the frontiers-man recognized that neither government nor armies would save them from hostile

forces, e.g., Indians; they had to depend upon themselves (p. 205). He maintains that this was particularly clear to the frontiersman in the valley of Virginia. "It was here that the people of the border began first to recognize their identity as a separate people and to realize that every relief or advantage they sought was to be gained by their own exertions" (p. 301). This was reinforced, he suggests, by the distances they traveled from former homes and associations, and by the fact that, given their geographical situation, they could not expect help from the military. According to Every, the cultural diversity among the frontier settlers also made them more prone to rely upon themselves than their neighbors.

35. Allen, p. 117.

36. Josephson, p. VIII.

37. Robert L. Heilbroner, *The Making of Economic Society*, 6th ed. (Englewood Cliffs, New Jersey: Prentice Hall, 1980), pp. 108, 109.

38. Thomas C. Cochran and William Miller, *The Age of Enterprise: A Social History of Industrial America*, rev. ed. (New York: Harper and Row, 1961), p. 129.

39. Stewart H. Holbrook, *The Age of the Moguls* (New York: Doubleday and Co., 1953), pp. IX–X.

40. Josephson, p. 315.

41. Holbrook, p. VIII.

42. Learner distinguishes between those robber barons who were deeply influenced by Puritan values and those he calls "magnifico." Of the former type he says, "They were probably closer than the magnificos to the theological roots of capitalism: the demonstration of virtue through success, the doctrine of calling, the gospel of work and thrift." Max Learner, *America as a Civilization*, vol. 1 (New York: Simon and Schuster, A Clarion Book, 1967), p. 278. The later type include "titans" such as Jay Gould, John W. Gates, Hill and John Pierpont Morgan. They gambled, were models of conspicuous consumption, and generally "operated on a scale of magnificence" (p. 278). Learner offers the following interesting generalization about these titans. "Together these two strains condense the appeal of business enterprise as a way of life. To the middle-class mind the appeal is to the Puritan virtues of austerity and acquisitiveness, to the Faustian spirit of the imaginative it is that of movers and shakers and of empire builders.... Neither is complete without

the other, and while in every Titan one or the other had predominated, no Titan has lacked elements of both" (pp. 278–279).

43. Thorstein Veblen, *The Theory of The Leisure Class* (New York: Mentor Book, 1953), pp. 154, 159.

44. For example, Fine says, "Carnegie was saying that the promotion of the general welfare of the community should be entrusted to those who had managed to make the most money rather than to the representatives of the people. Identifying wealth with intelligence, he insisted that the millionaires would know better than the people's government how to expend funds for the common good." Sidney Fine, *Laissez Faire and the General-welfare State* (Ann Arbor: the University of Michigan Press, 1956), p. 116. Fine relates this to the Protestant ethic. "Carnegie's Gospel of Wealth accorded perfectly with Protestant ideas of stewardship" (p. 120).

45. Adams, pp. 269–270. Josephson says, "The excitement of empire building and destroying had gripped them like a powerful drug…; but it had not prepared them in any sense for an art of leisure, or for cultivated intercourse with each other…. Few of them knew how to talk, or knew what to do with themselves. Perhaps one or two individuals in all the crowd, a Henry Villard or a William C. Whitney, possessed education or were innately cultured" (Josephson, p. 335).

46. For a development of this, see John G. Cawelti, *Apostles of the Self-Made Man* (Chicago: University of Chicago Press, 1965), pp. 167–199.

47. Cawelti, pp. 181–183.

48. Josephson says the following about the influence of the robber barons on higher education. "Now as the overlords of beef, department stores, banks and especially of railroads began to assume leadership in educational affairs—though almost none of them, except Pierpont Morgan, ever boasted a university education—a revolution in policy was effected which is generally pictured as the triumph of technology and applied science over the classical humanities" (Josephson, p. 324).

49. Milton Friedman, *Capitalism and Freedom* (Chicago: The University of Chicago Press, 1962), pp. 133–134.

50. Fine, writing about this period, says, "The success of the businessman, it was explained, was the result of possessing certain simple virtues and abilities; the failure of the poor man resulted from his lack of these same virtues and abilities" (Fine, p. 98). He continues, "Not only did the businessman equate success with

virtue and concentration, but he sought to impress upon one and all the view that there was ample room at the top for those who were willing to make the effort. 'The storehouse of opportunity is open to all,' proclaimed Benjamin Wood" (Fine, p. 98).

51. See, for example, Pitirim Sorokin, *Social Mobility* (New York: Harper, 1926) and Seymour M. Lipset and Reinhard Bendix, *Social Mobility in Industrial Society* (Berkeley: University of California Press, 1963). Quoting Carl Degler, Alan Trachtenburg says, "The men who were getting to the top...even in the 1870's—that alleged era of the self-made man—had not been poor farm boys or uneducated immigrant lads starting at the bottom, but instead men who had been given rather exceptional opportunities to make the race to the top." *The Incorporation of America: Culture and Society in the Gilded Age* (New York: Hill and Wang, 1982), p. 79.

52. For a discussion of this doctrine, see Richard Hofstadter, *Social Darwinism in American Thought*, rev. ed. (Boston: Beacon Press, 1944).

53. Fine, pp. 99–100. Similarly, Cochran and Miller maintain, "To a generation singularly engrossed in the competitive pursuit of industrial wealth it [the philosophy of Herbert Spencer] gave cosmic sanction to free competition. In an age of science, it 'scientifically' justified ceaseless exploitation. Precisely attuned to the aspirations of American businessmen, it afforded them a guide to faith and thought perfectly in keeping with the pattern of their workaday lives. When they were hopeful, it was infinitely optimistic; when they were harsh, it 'proved' that harshness was the only road to progress.... Their cupidity, it defended as part of the universal struggle for existence; their wealth, it hallowed as the sign of the 'fittest'" (Cochran and Miller, p. 119).

54. Thus, for example, Cochran and Miller maintain that Spencer's theory was rejected by both professional philosophers and scientists.

55. Ferdinand Schevill, *The Medici* (New York: Harper and Row, 1960), p. 57.

56. Col. G. F. Young, C. B. *The Medici* (New York: The Modern Library, 1930), p. 41. Cf. J. R. Hale, *Florence and the Medici: The Pattern of Control* (Great Britain: Thames and Hudson, 1977), p. 13.

57. Young, p. 46. Schevill mentions Cosimo's "unrivaled success" as a merchant (p. 104). He says, "Possessed of shrewd caution and bold initiative in happy

unison, he succeeded in so enlarging its [the Medici bank] operations, that it became the leading institution of its kind in the western world" (p. 104).

58. Young, p. 76. Schevill argues that "the interests that mainly shaped his [Cosimo's] mind were business and politics" (p. 67).

59. As quoted in Young, p. 56.

60. Schevill says, "Though the son of a merchant destined to a merchant's career, he was given express instruction in classical literature by several of its adepts. It thus came about that...he nursed a genuine interest in the movement. This, strengthened by innumerable personal contacts, cast him for the role of patron of the new learning, a role his wealth then permitted him to play in the lavish manner of a great prince" (p. 86).

61. Burckhardt says, "To Cosimo belongs the special glory of recognizing in the Platonic philosophy the fairest flower of the ancient world of thought, of inspiring his friends with the same belief, and, thus, of fostering within humanistic circles another and a higher rebirth of antiquity." Jacob Burckhardt, *The Civilization of the Renaissance in Italy* (New York: Mentor, 1960), p. 171.

62. Schevill, p. 107.

63. Schevill, p. 107.

64. Young, p. 150.

65. Young, p. 151.

66. Francesco Guicciardini, *The History of Florence*, trans. Mario Domandi (New York: Harper and Row, 1970), p. 73. Cf. Cecilia M. Ady, *Lorenzo Dei Medici and Renaissance Italy* (London: The English Universities Press LTD., 1960), pp. 39–41.

67. Guicciardini, p. 73. Cf. Christopher Hubbert, *The House of Medici: Its Rise and Fall* (New York: Morrow Quill Paperbacks, 1980), pp. 158–159.

68. Schevill, p. 118.

69. Schevill, p. 141.

70. Schevill, p. 165.

71. Thus, referring to Guicciardini's remarks (Probably, Guicciardini, p. 69), Young says, "Nor did political affairs, literature, and art absorb the whole of Lorenzo's attention, for under his rule 'all industries, commerce, and public works made enormous progress'" (p. 192). Again, referring to Guicciardini, Young mentions how Lorenzo's efforts to keep Italy at peace were instrumental in achieving the

most prosperous conditions that Italy had experienced for a thousand years (p. 196). Ady agrees: "In those happy days [the Laurentian age], Florence was united and at peace, there was full employment and an abundant food supply; the wealth of the merchants and their cultivated tastes gave every opportunity for the development of talent, and throughout Italy the city was renowned as never before" (p. 86).

72. Schevill, p. 168. We have seen that the above Medici were known for their humane rule. Schevill says that unlike Lorenzo's counterparts in Italy, "he interpreted the humanism to which he was devoted not only as a new and stimulating form of intellectuality but also as a nobler social order, under which the surviving remnants of feudal barbarism would be replaced by a code of softer and more urbane relationships. He was therefore, although exercising a form of tyranny, a ruler eminently humane and free from rancor" (pp. 166–7).

73. See, for example, Young, p. 151 and Guicciardini, p. 71. Ady intimates that one should take a broad view of Lorenzo as a "man of business." She suggests that Lorenzo's ability to make political friends was instrumental in developing contacts (e.g., Innocent VIII, King Ferrante, and Tommaso Portinari) which helped the Medici bank to revive during Lorenzo's later years (p. 42).

74. See, for example, Howard M. Jones, *O Strange New World: American Culture: The Formative Years* (New York: The Viking Press, 1964), pp. 196, 198.

CHAPTER III

AMERICAN BUSINESS VALUES PART II
POSTDEPRESSION AMERICAN BUSINESS VALUES

I have argued that traditional American business values leave much to be desired from the moral point of view. Historically, the Great Depression put an end to the unlimited faith in American business individualism. An analysis of the benefits and deficiencies of this value system could have produced modifications which would have moderated its evils while maximizing the benefits. Instead, as is too often the case when thoughtless reaction substitutes for reflection about one's values, the erosion of business individualism gave rise to the opposite ethic which William H. Whyte calls the "social ethic"—the ethic of the organization man.[1]

1. The Development of The Organization Man

There were a number of factors which helped to undermine the dominance of the traditional American individualistic ethic. Modern economic organizations in the United States are built upon specialization. Whether we consider an automobile factory with its assembly line or a corporation, some whole of relative complexity is broken down into parts, and a person's work is specialized and relative to these "parts." Psychologically, the significance of one's career as an employee of a modern organization, and in some cases one's life, is seen in terms of being a small part of some larger whole which one does not fully understand. This tends to substitute a sense of belongingness for a sense of individuality. The bureaucratic nature of American business organizations reinforces this deemphasis on individuality. The following are some other factors which have tended to support the development of the character type Whyte calls the organization man. The intensification of materialism created a dominant desire for comfort, ease (passivity), and security. This tended to erode the concern for self-reliance, hard work, delayed gratification, and the like, which were fundamental to the ideal of American individualism. Although much lip service is paid to the concept of laissez-faire, it was business that pioneered the elimination of economic insecurity. Many psychologists—e.g., Karen Horney, Eric Fromm, Harry S. Sullivan—argue that the individualistic emphasis in American values led to increasingly impersonal relations which caused a sense of rootlessness accompanied by heightened feelings of insecurity, anxiety, and loneliness. This insecurity was intensified by the period of the Great Depression. In attempting to escape from these negative feelings, we search for belongingness and togetherness, the keynotes of the organization man. Possibly, also, many people feel that the modern world is too complex to comprehend. A desire for excessive belongingness and togetherness may, in part, be the result of the attempt to escape from having to face problems felt to be too complex to be solved by individuals. Business, both from the side of management and labor, in the modern business world, has tended to create a paternalism, or at least the appearance of one, rather than perpetuate old-fashioned American individualism. The paternalism on the part of the modern corporation is based upon the recognition that enlightened self-interest requires such an attitude, while, on the part of labor, it was, of course, developed by the spread of unionism.

Whyte emphasizes two factors, related to the intellectual world, which helped to undermine traditional American individualism. He says, "William James, John Dewey, Charles Beard, Thorstein Veblen, the muckrakers and a host of reformers brought...the Protestant Ethic under relentless fire, and in so doing helped lay the groundwork for the Social Ethic."[2] Pragmatism, for example, with its emphasis on social utility, helped to provide "an intellectual framework for organizational growth."[3] Whyte also argues that the popularity of social engineering, with its emphasis on eliminating conflict between an organization and individuals, helped to reinforce the importance of belongingness; the rejection of belongingness at least necessitates the acceptance of conflict and change.

We have considered major factors leading to the development of an organization man mentality in American business. This character type was analyzed in some depth by Whyte in *The Organization Man*. Whyte describes the social ethic (the ethic of the organization man) in the following way:

> Man exists as a unit of society. Of himself, he is isolated, meaningless; only as he collaborates with others does he become worth while, for by sublimating himself in the group, he helps produce a whole that is greater than the sum of its parts. There should be, then, no conflict between man and society. What we think are conflicts are misunderstandings, breakdowns in communication. By applying the methods of science to human relations, we can eliminate these obstacles to consensus and create an equilibrium in which society's needs and the needs of the individual are one and the same.[4]

According to Whyte, three basic ideas are involved in the above quotation—belongingness, togetherness, and the application of scientific methodology and scientific ideas to business. I shall emphasize the first two as basic.

The concept of belongingness (in a corporation) is described in the following way: Such a corporation provides "an environment in which everyone is tightly knit into a belongingness with one another; one in which there is no restless wondering, but rather the deep emotional security that comes from total integration with the group."[5] The organization man sees no conflict between the individual and the group—what is good for the group is good for the individual. Therefore, the individual should adjust to the organization, leaving its basic goals unquestioned; only the techniques for reaching these goals should be evaluated. Unorthodoxy is seen as dangerous to the organization and, therefore, conformity is one of its keynotes. Seeing himself as a part of some organizational whole, he derives a sense of place, stability, and security from the firm. There is a trust in the beneficence of the organization which breeds loyalty. What is needed, according to this view, is an administrative elite who recognizes that what people really want most is group solidarity, and they will "adjust" people to this environment by social engineering, i.e., psychological conditioning techniques applicable to industrial psychology. The father of modern social engineering is B. F. Skinner.

The organization man not only wants to belong; he wants to function in this context of belongingness by working with others in a group. This togetherness manifests itself in an emphasis on such concepts as team work and committee work rather than individual effort. Bureaucracy, Whyte suggests, entails the "committee way." It also involves the notion of being a team player and therefore, according to Whyte, conformity rather than individuality.

Whyte does not believe that committees function as creatively as individuals; people, he suggests, rarely think in a group, and the emphasis on consensus often inhibits creativity. Given the value system of the organization man, Whyte has good reasons for his view. But it is not necessarily correct that individuals function more creatively than groups. If a group leader encourages thinking, analogous to a philosophy teacher using the Socratic method with a class of bright students, the group should produce helpful ideas. Of course, such an atmosphere discourages, rather than encourages, conformity.

Second, I do not think that Whyte clearly understands the notion of American conformism. Although the fear that traditional American individualism is being replaced by the ethic of the organization man is based in fact, Whyte seems to assume, incorrectly, that American individualism and conformity are entirely different concepts. Historically, American conformism existed side by side with American individualism. A Jacksonian democrat was a conformist in values, yet he was a frontiersman. Tocqueville's American is an individualist whose values were governed by peer or majority pressure; that is, he or she is a conformist. Tocqueville's American and Turner's American individualist are not antithetical to each other. American individualism emphasizes self-reliance and self-sufficiency, but this is compatible with a people that tends to conform to certain values. Nonetheless, it is clear that the postdepression American businessperson is considerably less individualistic than his predepression counterpart, and predepression American conformism is not characterized by Whyte's notion of belongingness.

Whyte admits that a social ethic has value, especially where individualism is carried to the extreme of preventing effective cooperation. But he believes that this ethic, as the new dominant corporate one replacing the old individualistic Protestant ethic, saps our resistance to imposed organizational values. The Protestant ethic maintains that success is due to character rather than luck or environmental factors. Corporate bureaucracy undermines this and makes people feel that they are objects acted upon and, therefore, determined by the system.[6] The conflict for the executive with integrity is apparent.

Of all the organization men the true executive is the one who remains most suspicious of The Organization. If there is one thing that characterizes him, it is a fierce desire to control his own destiny and deep down, he resents yielding that control to The Organization.[7]

But Whyte seems to think that this view is more prevalent among older executives. He says, "So far I have been arguing that the older executive is far more suspicious of organization than the professional manager who is the model of the next generation of management."[8] Whyte apparently believes that middle management takes most readily to the idea of the organization man. "Of all the people in organizational life, they [middle management] are best able to reconcile their own modest aspirations with the demands of organization. But the most able are not vouchsafed this solace."[9]

I agree with Whyte that there are distinct dangers associated with the concept of belongingness. Indeed, as he suggests, some of the more dangerous aspects of this concept as it applies to organizational life relate to the putative paternalism of modern organizations. Medieval life was characterized by this notion of belongingness. It was based upon a philosophy of organism—the parts exist to serve the whole. Thus, according to Thomas Aquinas, people stand to the community as parts to the whole. The community precedes the individual in importance. The medieval church provided a model for this view, but in its passion for oneness, it often oppressed individual faith. Traditional Japanese society is based upon a philosophy of organism. Division of labor, the heart of industrialization and the modern corporation, as I suggested, functions well under this concept since the parts (workers doing specialized jobs) exist to serve the whole, the corporation.[10] No wonder Japanese capitalism functions so well; it does not have our fierce individualistic traditions to cause conflicts.[11]

The great communities imagined by Christianity, or even, for example, by the Stoic or utopian philosophers, were communities in which the individual could identify himself or herself as a whole person. The corporation, however, dismembers a person by dividing the whole into parts and forcing a person to shrink to one part of himself. There is, therefore, a distinct danger in taking seriously the claim of a paternalistic firm to meet our needs as if the corporation were one big family.

The difficulty is that it is not, and cannot be, a family. Many paternalistic firms work on a theory of enlightened self-interest. Developing a paternalistic image for a firm not only caters to the security and stability needs of employees, it helps reduce the possibility of government regulation and public criticism and, more positively, creates public good will by enhancing the public image of the corporation. However, it is dangerous to depend upon the generosity of corporations. I shall return to this problem in Chapter 6. Whyte, himself, emphasizes the dangers of corporate paternalism. He argues that a basic danger of organizational life is its very benevolence. This tends to rob the individual of his defenses. In cases of conflict or potential conflict, the organization, he correctly suggests, will look to its own interests or to the individual's interests only as the organization interprets them.

2. Other Thinkers on The Organization Man

Analyses of the organization man were prevalent among intellectuals in the 1950's. For example, David Riesman's *Lonely Crowd* develops the concept of the other-directed personality. This type of person, typified by the bureaucrat, underscores an important psychological feature of the organization man, his need to conform to group stimuli. For this person, one's peers are the source of guiding life principles.[12] Riesman emphasizes the fact that this person does not merely tend to conform in externals or appearance; more importantly, he conforms "in the quality of his inner experience."[13] The other-directed person's antennas are always out for cues as to "correct" behavior.

One interesting feature of Riesman's analysis, which is unfortunately absent from Whyte's, is his concern with the shift away from emphasis on craftsmanship which he attributes to the pressure toward social rather than technical competence required by "American business and professional life." As people progress up the hierarchical ladder of bureaucracies, they must "bury their craft routines and desert their craft companions."[14] He says, "A society increasingly dependent on manipulation of people is almost as destructive of the craft-oriented professional and businessman as a society in the earlier stages of industrialism is destructive of the handicraft-oriented peasant and artisan."[15] He argues that the glad-hander can rediscover some "inner-directed" resources through craftsmanship, but there is a danger in romanticizing the past, for it cannot be recovered. "What we need," he suggests, "is a reinterpretation which will allow us to focus on individual character development."[16] In chapter 6, I shall attempt a "reinterpretation" of individualism based upon a concept which I call generic craftsmanship; this type of individualism allows a person to recover a healthy "inner-directedness" and helps to develop a virtuous character. A craftsman, whose concern is the creation of something excellent, looks to himself or herself—the development of one's abilities. A concern for personal satisfaction, pride in accomplishment, and dignity substitute for extrinsic values. Self-worth is based upon self-development rather than the other-directed concerns of the organization man. Moreover, as I shall argue in Chapter 6, a craftsmanship type of self-interest relates to a concern for one's own dignity and worth, and with proper nurturing, such self-interest can be extended to include a concern for the development of other people's potentialities. A craftsmanship ethic, then, can be developed which is essentially nonmanipulative.

Eric Fromm, in *Man for Himself* and other works, develops the concept of the marketing-oriented personality. This character type, he says, "is rooted in the experience of oneself as a commodity and of one's value as exchange value."[17] Thus, this person molds himself into a marketable personality. Like Riesman's other-directed personality (which was influenced by Fromm's character type), the marketing-oriented person is sensitive to cues concerning what is fashionable or most in demand; he is totally adaptable to people's changing expectations. Basically, he is a careerist in the sense that he defines himself in terms of his career. His success, then, is determined by his acceptability. He molds his traits into a "personality package" that sells. His sense of value, therefore, is contingent upon that which is out of his control; he feels no inner core he can call "himself." Like Peer Gynt (Henrik Ibsen) he is similar to "an onion with layer after layer, and without a kernel."[18]

Since Fromm defines this character type as one who is infinitely flexible given "market" variations, one might think that this type is fundamentally different from the one Whyte analyzes. Security is essential to the organization man; yet the success of the marketing-oriented person, and his feelings of esteem, depend on what is beyond his control and, therefore, his feelings of insecurity are acute. This, however, is not true. Whyte, we saw, says that the organization man is like an object acted upon and determined by outside forces. Moreover, Fromm recognizes the intense desire that modern man has for economic and emotional security. "Increasingly people feel that they should have no doubts, no problems, that they should have to take no risks, and that they should always feel 'secure'."[19] The marketing-oriented personality fits this goal well, for modern man feels secure by conforming, by being like his peers; his primary goal is gaining approval.[20] Second, in the modern world, Fromm thinks, the opportunities for the individualist are much less than what they were. "He who wants to get ahead has to fit into large organizations, and his ability to play the expected role is one of his main assets."[21] Modern business requires people with standardized tastes who must "cooperate smoothly in large groups." This requires people who are willing "to do what is expected, to fit into the social machine without force."[22] That is, what is required is the marketing-oriented person.

Fromm's analysis of the marketing-oriented personality gives us some important psychological insights into the organization man. He is a fundamentally alienated individual; a manipulator who is himself manipulated like a commodity. Since he has, as Fromm says, no inner core, no individuality, he and his relationships with others are superficial; indeed, he understands neither himself nor others. He may be bright, but only in a superficial sense; his intelligence serves manipulative purposes but does not dip below the surface in order to understand things in depth. What counts is on the surface, the "looks" of people and things, rather than the reality. As a worker, he is alienated from the source of creative labor, craftsmanship, and like Riesman's other-directed type, his character is destructive of craftsmanship.[23] For Fromm, a deemphasis on skills and craftsmanship is a consequence of overemphasizing personality, the hallmark of the marketing-oriented person.

The marketing-oriented personality is also analyzed by C. Wright Mills. In *White Collar*, he says what many corporate employees feel about their firms.

> The success literature has shifted with the success pattern. It is
> still focused upon personal virtues, but they are not the sober
> virtues once imputed to successful entrepreneurs. Now the stress
> is on agility rather than ability, on 'getting-along'...; on who

you know rather than what you know; on techniques of self-display and the generalized knack of handling people, rather than on moral integrity, substantial accomplishments, and solidity of person; on loyalty to, or even identity with, one's own firm rather than on entrepreneurial virtuosity.[24]

The basic factor, says Mills, is personality—be courteous, smile, act alert, radiate self-confidence. One should get the attention of the higher ups by being dependable and enthusiastic about one's job. Sell and keep selling yourself. For Mills, this character model is devoid of character. No longer are materialistic ends justified as signs of virtue, as they were in predepression America. "In the white-collar pattern," says Mills, "there is no such moral sanctifying of the means of success; one is merely prodded to become an instrument of success, to acquire tactics not virtues; money[-]success is assumed to be an obviously good thing for which no sacrifice is too great."[25]

Robert Jackall supports Mills's position. In analyzing the bureaucratic world of corporate managers, he argues that many executives do not see traditional individualistic values as leading to business success. "Instead of ability, talent, and dedicated service to an organization, politics, adroit talk, luck, connections, and self-promotion are the real sorters of people into sheep and goats."[26]

3. The Organization Man Ethic and Contemporary American Business

Many of the observers of the American business scene believe that this ethic, or some form of it, still plays an important part in American business, especially at the level of middle management. The organization man mentality is supported by business partly because big business desires to eliminate unplanned changes; this necessitates control over the business variables, and the most difficult variable to control is people. Business, then, favors uniformity and conformity and considers these characteristics to be prerequisites of organizational culture.

Whyte's thesis has been defended by William G. Scott and David K. Hart as a position which is still applicable to American corporations. They argue, as Whyte did, that psychological behavioral techniques are used by corporations for integration purposes. The corporation's goal is organizational health, and its criteria are growth, adaptability, and efficiency. Scott and Hart maintain that the criterion of organizational health has two important consequences. The first is that managers must be expedient, in fact, amoral, in order to obtain the most benefits for their organizations. Second, managers need not worry about their actions if they are expedient, for organizations shield them from public accountability.[27] The goal of organizational health is said to demand the organizational imperative—the good of the individual is said to be derived from the good of the organization (Whyte's concept of belongingness). The emphasis on the good of the organization necessitates the using of people as malleable substances that can be shaped and reshaped for maximum organizational utility, homogeneity of values, and the dispensability of people (people become as dispensable as the parts of a machine). "By adopting the organizational imperative as the foundation of personal values," they argue, "the agonies of introspection and the articulation of personal value commitments are removed and purpose is given to individual lives."[28] The conversion is painless, materially rewarding, and is praiseworthy in the eyes of the authorities. They give an example of a student who wanted his MBA program to stuff him like a sausage so that he would be digestible to his future employer—a perfect example of Fromm's marketing-oriented personality. Indeed, Scott and Hart implicitly show the relationship between Fromm's model and Whyte's. They suggest that as people flee more deeply into the organization searching for security, they find only that they are the most dispensable commodity of all. But this feeling of insecurity, as Fromm suggests, is implicit in the marketing-oriented model.

Jackall agrees that American bureaucratic business emphasizes expediency, manipulation, a concern for security, subordination of personal values (except ambition) to group values and the rationalization of compromises, and sycophantic activity in the relations between CEOs and subordinates. In a world where appearances are everything, he argues, the "wise," ambitious manager learns how to package himself; he molds himself after an image that will help him to survive and prosper in an organization. That is, he learns to be a marketing-oriented personality. He maintains, however, that although the conformity and team playing can be taken as marks of the organization man (and, consequently, of the decline of traditional American business individualism), it can also be looked at as basically the management of "public faces."[29] I have noted that Whyte, himself, suggests that not all organization men are true believers. But even if Jackall is correct and management is not taken in by an organizational imperative, its conduct will conform to that of the organization man; and, clearly, one's conduct, over time, molds one's character. It is common practice for management to act in accordance with organization man values while its talk is individualistic. John K. Galbraith, for example, says that modern corporate executives picture themselves as "self-reliant men…fiercely competitive and with a desire to live dangerously." "Individualism," according to Galbraith, "is the note that 'sounds through the business creed like the pitch in a Byzantine Choir'."[30]

4. The Moral Inadequacies of The Organization Man Ethic

What are the ethical consequences of the organization man ethic? The organization man's excessive desire for security, stability, conformity, and adjustment makes him incapable of understanding individualized effort, e.g., innovative, creative, and daring (risktaking) efforts. As managers, how can such people be just to those who exhibit individualistic traits required for business growth? Their appearance as caring people hides a basic lack of concern for others and a lack of depth in their relationships. The more extreme form of organization man is the true believer who sacrifices real virtue for the avoidance of the pain of moral conflict and moral search, and his extreme bureaucratic tendencies make this ethic, at its worst, repressive, lacking in idealism, insensitive, and destructive of the individual. But, nonetheless, even if Jackall is correct and the modern manager is not this true believer, the modern manager sacrifices personal morality for expediency and is blind to his own self-manipulation. Generally, the organization man ethic tends to erode our courage and integrity and forces moral decisions into a conventional mode—one governed by majority opinion and motivated by concern for rewards and fear of punishment (the carrot and the stick). His morality is reduced to a superficial concern with manners, and there is no real commitment to self-development or to anything that gives quality to life. In reducing a person to something less than he ought to be, morality is reduced to something less than it ought to be.

5. Predictable Changes in Managerial Values: The Gamesman

In Chapter 1, I mentioned that the analysis conducted in Chapters 2 and 3 is important for the following reasons. First, it is indispensable for understanding the moral inadequacies of modern American business. The common type of pessimism related to business morality (which will be discussed in Appendix I) is superficial compared to the deeper understanding of the moral deficiencies of American business uncovered by our analysis. Second, I suggested that the discussion in Chapters 2 and 3 is most helpful in determining possible ways of developing a business ethic that accords well with our moral sensibilities. As I said, in order to find solutions, one must understand what the problems are. Logically, solutions to superficial problems are superficial solutions. Both this and the previous chapter help us to understand the basic moral inadequacies of American business. In the following two chapters, I shall develop these inadequacies by providing a Platonic critique of managerial leadership insofar as it incorporates American business values. This critique will help us to evaluate American business leadership from the standpoint of viable virtue criteria. With such an evaluation and some reasonable standards for virtue, we shall be in a better position to find some sort of solution to the problems of business statesmanship and a moral organization. I shall attempt such a solution in Chapter 6. In addition to the above considerations, the analysis in Chapters 2 and 3 should help to determine potential or future changes in managerial character types. I shall now illustrate this point.

If the organization man ethic dominates corporate management, one can predict that, given basic changes in the environment—for example, economic or social changes—the organization man mentality would not be entrepreneurial enough to meet these challenges and organizational stagnation will set in. Where would management look to counteract such stagnation? Since people's conduct is most often determined by their culture, there will be, at least, an unconscious appeal to traits exhibited in American business culture. This, it would seem, is what happened in American management in the 1970's. Changes in management styles readily result from new combinations of traditional ethics which are formed, at least unconsciously, to meet present business needs. According to Michael Maccoby, the character model that dominated the upper echelons of management in the 1970's is the gamesman. This model appears to be a combination of the robber baron (winning is the basic goal and this is achieved by being tough, aggressive, taking calculated risks, manifesting great energy, innovativeness, being unafraid of change, priding oneself on one's individuality, being contemptuous of weakness, and the like) and the organization man (being a team player, cooperative, dependent on the game and others in the organization, and deriving basic meaning in life from the organizational games played).[31] Many businesspeople believe that the growth of business in the 1970's depended upon the modification of the organization man's managerial style by that of traditional American business individualism. The gamesman seems to be the result. Some of the moral inadequacies of this character type are also predictable. Although Maccoby shows that the gamesman has positive moral traits (he is unprejudiced or fair, not destructive, does not relish defeating others and is not nasty or vindictive), the gamesman, like the robber baron of old, is basically unfeeling, unprincipled, and manipulative. He is not compassionate and generally is not motivated by issues related to social responsibility. The gamesman, therefore, is not a proper model for business statesmanship.

NOTES

1. William H. Whyte Jr., *The Organization Man* (New York: Simon and Schuster, 1956).
2. Whyte, p. 20.
3. Whyte, pp. 20–21.
4. Whyte, p. 7.
5. Whyte, p. 32.
6. Whyte, p. 395.
7. Whyte, p. 151.
8. Whyte, pp. 156–157.
9. Whyte, p. 151.
10. See, for example, Shuji Hayashi, *Culture and Management in Japan*, trans. Frank Baldwin (Tokyo: University of Tokyo Press, 1988), pp. 67–81.

11. De Mente maintains that the Japanese businessman, as a reflection of his culture, is the model organization man. "His dread of personal responsibility; his preference for mutual operation and group effort; his tendency to follow the mass and to imitate success; his reluctance to oppose anyone openly; his desire to submerge his individualism into his surroundings, etc. As a result of his conditioning, he is and has been for over a thousand years the nearly perfect Organization Man." Boye De Mente, *Japanese Etiquette and Ethics in Business* (Lincolnwood, Ill.: NTC Publishing Co., 1990), p. 41.

12. David Riesman with Nathan Glazer and Reuel Denny, *The Lonely Crowd: A Study of the Changing American Character*, abridged ed. (New Haven: Yale University Press, 1961), pp. 20–21.

13. Riesman, p. 24.

14. Riesman, p. 129.

15. Riesman, pp. 130–131.

16. Riesman, p. 297.

17. Erich Fromm, *Man for Himself: An Inquiry into the Psychology of Ethics* (New York: Holt, Rinehart and Winston, 1947), p. 68.

18. Erich Fromm, *The Sane Society*, (New York: Holt, Rinehart and Winston, 1955), p. 143. Fromm's term "marketing-oriented personality" has its Japanese counterpart in the phrase *"jibunganai"*—"I have no self." De Mente says that Japanese, especially those born before 1950, "tend to have shallow and fragile concepts of themselves as individual entities" (De Mente, p. 113). Thus, although the Japanese are ambitious and success-oriented, the emphasis is on the success of the group rather than the individual.

19. Fromm, p. 195.

20. Fromm, pp. 196–197.

21. Fromm, *Man for Himself*, p. 82.

22. Fromm, *The Sane Society*, p. 110.

23. Fromm, p. 178.

24. C. Wright Mills, *White Collar* (New York: Oxford University Press, 1956), p. 263.

25. Mills, p. 265.

26. Robert Jackall, *Moral Mazes: The World of Corporate Managers* (New York: Oxford University Press, 1988), p. 3.

27. William G. Scott and David K. Hart, *Organizational America* (Boston: Houghton Mifflin Co., 1979), pp. 37–38.

28. Scott and Hart, pp. 64–65.

29. Jackall, p. 61.

30. John K. Galbraith, *The New Industrial State* (New York: Signet Books, 1967), p. 103. Capitman says, "Today *the glorification* of entrepreneurship continues, even though there is currently little place for entrepreneurial behavior. Small businesses are more likely to be unsuccessful than successful. Success and achievement in American life today go to the man whom William H. Whyte describes as the 'organization man'—one who establishes himself in the bosom of corporate or governmental bureaucracy, and by persistence and narrowness moves up the sharply defined steps of the ladder." William G. Capitman, *Panic in the Boardroom* (New York: Anchor Books, 1975), p. 65.

31. See Michael Maccoby, *The New Corporate Leaders: The Gamesman* (New York: Simon and Schuster, 1976).

CHAPTER IV

A PLATONIC CRITIQUE OF AMERICAN BUSINESS LEADERSHIP
PART I
PLATO'S *STATESMAN* AND BUSINESS LEADERSHIP: AN ANALYSIS FROM AN ETHICAL POINT OF VIEW

In this chapter, I shall show that Plato's model of leadership (statesmanship) in the *Statesman*, most importantly the "weaving" of temperate and courageous qualities in leaders, is a very useful model for analyzing business leadership, especially from an ethical standpoint. The history of American business values reveals the generally destructive effects of deviating from this model. Specifically, I shall argue that the development of the American business character from the colonial period to the Great Depression of the 1930's exhibits the moral difficulties of overemphasizing qualities ordinarily associated with courage, while postdepression organization man values in American business manifest the moral difficulties of overemphasizing traits associated with temperance. Courage and temperance, for Plato, are the basic moral virtues. Insofar as they presuppose Platonic wisdom, they are the virtues that make justice possible.[1] Therefore, I shall attempt to show that the virtues that follow from traditional and organization man values are really pseudo-virtues measured by a proper standard of virtue. (In Chapter 1, I argued that, according to Plato, a virtue must benefit both the individual and society.)

1. The Art of Statesmanship and Its Basic Problem

According to Plato, in the *Statesman*, qualities that are constituents of characters called temperate and courageous conflict and, therefore, so do the characters that manifest these conflicting forms of virtue. Temperate people are noted for their moderation and modesty and exhibit peaceloving qualities such as tranquility (quietness), stability (steadiness), and gentleness. Such people, says Plato, are excessively cautious, stick to precedents, but are fair. Courageous people, on the other hand, are noted for their acuteness and aggressiveness or "strong" action; they are vigorous, full of energy or drive, and exhibit more warlike traits such as boldness or daring. Such people, says Plato, are not cautious, not particularly fair, but they are effective—they get things done.

When the traits of either of these character types are taken to their extremes and embodied in leaders, virtue turns into vice and these leaders of organized wholes such as cities cause their destruction. The passion for the peaceloving traits creates a person of "soft" character whose cowardice and sluggishness make one incapable of responding to the challenges of life, putting the city at "the mercy of the...aggressor."[2] The passion for the more warlike traits, on the other hand, results in destruction and devastation (violence and madness), for such militancy (excessive competitiveness) creates continual conflicts, e.g., with other cities, ultimately leading to the same result that is effected by "soft" leadership—the destruction of one's own city.

Ideally, the contrary qualities of temperate and courageous types should be combined in statesmen who have leadership positions, or statesmen, themselves, must bring together (harmonize) subordinate leaders who exhibit these conflicting character traits. The art of statesmanship, says Plato, is like the art of weaving.[3] The statesman must weave together "the firm warplike character" of the courageous type with the "supple, soft wooflike" character of the temperate type in such a way that the benefits of each type of character are secured while the deficiencies, manifested by extreme forms of either type, are eliminated.

The statesman's art of weaving is based upon knowledge of what is good and bad, just and unjust (proper values). Plato calls this the "divine bond," for it bonds together (weaves) traits of the above, opposed character types. The courageous type will be made a more gentle, just, and concerned citizen; without this, one becomes brutal or bestial. The temperate (peaceloving and orderly) nature becomes more moderate and prudent; without the "divine bond," one becomes foolish. The statesman, in applying the "divine bond," then, corrects the tendency to go to extremes of each temperamental type, and in so doing, is able to temper each type with qualities of the other type, i.e., weave together courageous and temperate properties. This can be seen, for example, if we note that an excess of courage (foolhardiness or rashness) entails intemperance or a lack of moderation and the tempering of this bias produces a more temperate nature, while an excess of temperance (too peaceloving and gentle a disposition) entails cowardice and the tempering of this bias produces a more courageous nature.

Implicit in the *Statesman* is the suggestion that the art of statesmanship—the royal art of weaving on the basis of knowing the "divine bond"—depends upon a knowledge of the correct mean between extremes (excess and defect), i.e., an ideal value standard that properly determines excess and defect.[4] This view was used by Aristotle, in the *Nicomachean Ethics*, to determine moral virtue and vice. Insofar as temperance and courage provide the basis for moral virtue, and they are properly woven together by applying the "divine bond," the doctrine of the mean indeed does, as Aristotle thought, provide the basis of the concept of moral virtue.

Having analyzed Plato's model for statesmanship (leadership), I shall apply, in the following two sections, the Platonic model to the history of American business values, as it was developed in Chapters 2 and 3.

2. Courage and American Business Predepression Values

Plato believes that the values that constitute our view of what is good, mold our character. It is therefore upon this basis that our moral judgments and character depend. For example, at the end of Book III of the *Republic*, Plato suggests that if the guardians become materialistic, the moral quality of their conduct, and consequently their character, will suffer. On this view, then, American business morality, or the lack of it, is intimately connected to basic American business values—to the American businessperson's conception of what is good. We have seen that American business predepression values are individualistic and materialistic. Postdepression American business values were seen to be dominated by some form of organization related values.

We have seen that American business individualistic-materialistic character models can be divided into three interrelated ethics which I called the Protestant, frontier, and robber baron ethics. As we progress historically from the former to the latter models, we saw that materialism becomes more extreme, while individualism (based upon self-reliance and self-sufficiency) becomes more cutthroat. For the purpose of applying the Platonic thesis, we can argue that during the predepression period the character traits of the so-called courageous type of person dominated, and with the development of the above three forms of the traditional American business ethic, the extreme of this type becomes more manifest leading to the immorality, not to mention the destruction of organized wholes, predicted by Plato.

The conception of individuality entailed by the Protestant ethic is not as extreme as that exhibited by the later American character types, i.e., the frontier and, especially, the robber baron ethics. Moreover, such virtues as orderliness, chastity, and temperance, emphasized by Benjamin Franklin, provided some moderating influence on this value system, and Calvinism, which supported business materialism, nonetheless did not allow Puritan materialism to develop to the extreme manifested by the robber barons. For example, no Puritan would have thought of practicing what Veblen called conspicuous consumption. From a moral point of view, however, we have seen that there are important criticisms that can be leveled against the Protestant ethic.

Puritan leaders believed that they were the stewards or the natural leaders of the people. But like their modern business counterparts who picture themselves as the productive members of society, Puritan merchants (especially by the second half of the 17th century) viewed their paternalism in a too narrowly materialistic manner. Proper leaders—for Plato the model leader is the philosopher-king or statesman who comprehends the "divine bond"—focus on the whole not on a truncated materialistic, too narrowly conceived individualistic view of human values. (This view will be developed in the next chapter.) Such Puritan leadership (based upon an inadequate conception of the "divine bond") foreshadows moral problems related to attitudes or values of the American businessperson. The attitude of the later Puritan merchants to cultural and liberal arts pursuits, and their view that material success is the sign of virtue and, therefore, a lack of such success is the sign of vice (discussed in Chapter 2) tend to dehumanize the courageous type of character implicit in the predepression value system.

The character traits attributed to the frontiersman, by Turner, illustrate the untempered traits Plato associates with the extreme courageous temperament.[5] Individualism became more narrowly selfish and materialism intensified. As we have said, lack of civic spirit and loose business morality were consequences of this intensified materialism.

The Protestant ethic (in the form adhered to by later Puritan merchants) with its deemphasis on cultural and liberal arts pursuits and its neglect of certain moral and social values, having been developed by the frontier experience, is taken to its extreme limits in the value system of the robber barons. This ethic illustrates the Platonic thesis concerning the destructive forces inherent in the courageous temperament; these forces are unleashed by allowing this temperament free rein and unlimited development (by neglecting to ground it in an adequate value system, i.e., a correct conception of the "divine bond").

Plato's prediction concerning the untempered development of the courageous character type proved correct in the history of the development of traditional American business values. Indeed, a reading of the pertinent sections of the *Statesman* will, I think, support the view that the robber baron character type is as clear a model of Plato's extreme courageous character as one might desire. Nonetheless, the character traits of the robber baron ethic—shrewdness, nerve (risk-taking), self-confidence, initiative, tremendous energy or drive, and the will to win at all costs—are much admired by the modern American businessperson.

Fierce competitiveness, ambition, self-confidence, and the ability to take risks, as I suggested, were forces driving these excessively spirited people. They saw themselves as the prime movers of human progress, and the world as a battlefield composed of winners (exploiters) and losers (exploited). Their view is well represented in Plato's *Republic*. Those who are competitive and unjust in a big way (as Thrasymachus in the *Republic* would say) rather than cooperative and just (Socrates) are the real winners; they gain wealth, glory, and power, the prizes of victory. Like Thrasymachus in the *Republic*, they distinguished between the men (tyrants) and the boys (conventional moral people). The former have the intelligence, manipulative skills, and courage to get what they desire; the latter do not and have to settle for justice as a compromise or necessary evil (cf. Glaucon in the *Republic*). Actually these predators (as Veblen called them) believed that they were just. As we saw, the myth of universal opportunities for advancement in America and Spencer's theory of Social Darwinism helped them to rationalize the misery and degradation that they were instrumental in producing. This latter theory made cutthroat competition into a virtue, and human degradation into a necessary byproduct of human progress.

Since the robber baron mentality is in evidence among American business-people, it should not be surprising that the robber baron ethic has influenced American business education. For example, according to Peter Cohen, in *The Gospel According to the Harvard Business School*, the Harvard B-School is 100% cutthroat.[6] The environment cultivates an aggressive, dog-eat-dog competitive, "hard and cold," and generally inhumane attitude. Students are motivated by fear, and the goal of education is winning, not learning. Students are examined and eliminated, not educated. Peers are viewed as potential enemies, and people as objects to be manipulated. The personal goals of the students are wealth and power. Given the positions such students will attain in business, the ethical prospects for business, not to mention for society in general, are frightening. The fact, as we have seen, that the business community has been guided by a value system steeped in an antiliberal arts, antihumane tradition argues for the importance of the type of analysis given in Chapters 2 and 3.

Maccoby, in *The Gamesman*, studies three other contemporary business character types besides the gamesman.[7] One of these types he calls the jungle fighter—a robber baron type. They are exponents of extreme individualism who believe that they have made it solely on their own. Like the traditional robber barons, they are addicted to the pursuit of wealth and power and use their cunning, daring, and strength to manipulate people for their own ends. Given their suspicious and distrustful attitude toward people, they function in a secretive, conspiratorial manner. Plato predicted the evils that would follow from allowing such people to have power. Although the jungle fighter is, at times, brought into a troubled corporation to rid it of its "dead wood," such a person eventually becomes a liability, because he or she creates hostility, distrust, and, generally, is destructive to the corporate community. Thus, as Plato suggests, such a character type eventually brings everyone down, including himself.

3. Temperance and American Business Postdepression Values

We saw that Plato, in the *Statesman*, argues that weaving and, by analogy, statecraft entail knowledge of the right measure or proportion between excess and defect; that is, knowledge of the mean. Marquis W. Childs and Douglass Cater argue that "In America the very concept of equilibrium, implying the Greek idea of balance, has somehow seemed alien to our tradition. Its achievement, therefore, has been all the more difficult."[8] Although they apply this to the difficulty of balancing Christian and business values, it also applies, generally, to the history of American business values. Instead of exhibiting the excesses of the courageous character type, many modern American businesspeople fit the type Plato would have characterized as excessively temperate. As Aristotle says, it is no easy task to discover and apply the mean between extremes.

We saw that Whyte and others lament a change in the American business character from an emphasis on individualism to that of a "social ethic"—the ethic of the organization man.[9] This character model can be seen to exhibit many of the traits Plato attributed to the extreme temperate type. Such a person, we saw, is addicted to peaceloving qualities such as tranquility (quietness) and gentleness. He, then, is excessively concerned with place, security, and stability. The extreme emphasis on peaceloving qualities, as Plato says, tends to create a person of soft character who lacks the assertiveness, boldness, and drive (energy) to respond to the challenges of life. Maccoby, in analyzing the contemporary counterpart he calls the company man, mentions similar character traits—his softness, lack of risktaking ability, lack of self-confidence, and dynamism. We mentioned that, in developing his picture of the excessively temperate character, Plato emphasizes the extreme modest and cautious traits of such people as well as their passion for sticking to precedents. Lacking self-confidence and daring, unable to innovate or be creative, this person, as I suggested in Chapter 3, is a conformist and a bureaucrat; he or she sticks to the rules, resists change, is motivated by the carrot and the stick (rewards and the avoidance of punishment), and is generally servile. Maccoby's analysis of the company man yields similar traits.

Plato argues that the lack of character of the extreme temperate type, in making such people incapable of responding to the challenges of life, puts the city at "the mercy of the... aggressor." A similar situation occurs with respect to the leadership of the organization man and the corporation. The organization man possesses certain traits that are favorable to the corporation. I suggested in the previous chapter that big business supports uniformity and conformity basically because it attempts to control business variables, and the most difficult of these variables to control is people. On the more positive side, Whyte's organization man is trustworthy, loyal, responsible, and, to some extent, capable of dedicating himself to some larger whole. Especially at the middle management level, he helps to maintain a certain stability within the organization. But because of the above mentioned character traits, he is incapable of innovating needed changes or meeting external challenges; he puts the corporation at "the mercy of...the aggressor." The overemphasis on stability leads to stagnation, and this provides a perfect atmosphere for his or her opposite number, the robber baron, to function, either in a take-over capacity or in the capacity of a cutthroat competitor.

4. Weaving Courageous and Temperate Traits: A Problem for American Business Leaders

It is relatively clear that the needs of modern big business require some sort of "weaving" of the individualistic traits of the traditional American business ethic and those of the more modern American business ethic. The destructiveness to the corporation and the negative moral effects of either robber baron or organization man leadership, as Plato would have reminded us, apparently necessitate a moderation of the extremes of both types and, ideally, a combination of the best traits of these opposing character models.

We saw that Maccoby argues that the dominant upper echelon corporate character model of the 1970's is the gamesman. This model, we recall, combines certain robber baron traits with specific organization man characteristics. Although this weaving process did moderate some of the more odious characteristics of the robber baron type (lust for power, lack of fairness, passion for knocking others down), Plato would have agreed with Maccoby that a proper balance or "right measure or proportion" has not been struck; that is, such a character is not "woven" on the basis of a correct conception of the "divine bond."

Although as modern corporate leaders, gamesmen are more successful than robber barons, if we are to believe the management theorists of what has been called the Stanford School, they are not the typical leaders of the most successful modern corporations. These theorists would argue that they are not sufficiently people-oriented. Like the robber baron, they are neither compassionate nor generous; in an unprincipled fashion, they will manipulate others for the sake of winning the "game."

The question remains as to whether these popular management theorists of the 1980's can provide any aid. An examination of their theories, I think, will help us to apply a Platonic model to corporations and provide a more adequate solution than that of the gamesman—or, for that matter, any of the other major character models exhibited in the history of American business culture—to the problem of developing a model which exhibits a proper "weave" of our two conflicting and inadequate character types. In Chapter 6, I shall especially appeal to Thomas J. Peters and Robert H. Waterman Jr.'s *In Search of Excellence*, to help develop a more adequate ethical model for business statesmanship.[10]

NOTES

1. Plato's analysis, in the *Republic*, of these four ancient Greek cardinal virtues will be considered in the next chapter.

2. *Statesman* 307e.

3. The weaving analogy is developed in the *Statesman* 305e–311c.

4. See *Statesman* 283c–284d.

5. Frederick J. Turner, *The Significance of the Frontier in American History* (Ann Arbor: University Microfilms Inc., 1966).

6. Peter Cohen, *The Gospel According to the Harvard Business School* (Baltimore: Penguin Books, 1973).

7. Michael Maccoby, *The New Corporate Leaders: The Gamesman* (New York: Simon and Schuster, 1976).

8. Marquis W. Childs and Douglass Cater, *Ethics in A Business Society* (New York: Mentor Books, 1954), p. 83.

9. William H. Whyte Jr., *The Organization Man* (New York: Simon and Schuster, 1956).

10. Thomas J. Peters and Robert H. Waterman Jr., *In Search of Excellence: Lessons from America's Best-Run Companies* (New York: Harper and Row, 1982).

CHAPTER V

A PLATONIC CRITIQUE OF AMERICAN BUSINESS LEADERSHIP PART II
PLATONIC *PAIDEIA* AND BUSINESS STATESMANSHIP

In the previous chapter, I argued that the *Statesman* provides a useful model for analyzing business leadership, viz., the weaving of temperate and courageous qualities in business leaders, and it is also helpful in criticizing pre and postdepression American business character models. However, we have not exhausted ethical criticism of American business from a Platonic point of view.

The education of Platonic business statesmen provides these leaders with an understanding of the values that ought to guide a business organization as a whole—values which provide maximum benefit for stakeholders and not merely stockholders. From this perspective, a critique of American business leadership should stress the negative effects of a too narrow economics orientation towards business, an overemphasis on specialization, and a deemphasis of the liberal arts. Generally, a Platonic critique of business leadership from an ethical point of view should uncover business values that are harmful to the human soul because they destroy human virtue—wisdom, courage, temperance, and justice. This chapter is devoted to a consideration of these issues and will complete my Platonic critique of American business leadership.

1. Business Statesmanship

The successful businessperson has been much admired by Americans. "It is no exaggeration," says Howard Laski, "to say that in no previous civilization has the businessman enjoyed either the power or the prestige that he possesses in the United States."[1] Like the paternal head of the family, he often views himself as society's material provider. Just as the material health of a family is essential for its stability, so the stability of a country is based upon its economic health. People, then, depend upon business for the type of leadership that secures their basic needs and provides for the foundation of the American dream. A prime requisite for such leadership, according to conventional wisdom, is strength; in the "real world" it is said that the softer sentiments related to morality do not lead to success. Rather, it is force or might that prevails. Thus, the good guy finishes last; he may be well liked, but he is not CEO material.

The analogy between the family's father and the corporate father tends to break down, because the family's father (or mother) is looked up to for moral as well as economic leadership, while businesspeople have not been noted, traditionally, for their moral leadership—the modern business executive's thinking is often essentially financial. Therefore, while the strong father is admired for the protection or security he provides, the strong business leader is looked upon with more ambivalence. For while his strength is necessary for the protection of the corporate family, there are doubts about his concern for this so-called family, and these doubts persist no matter how much he attempts to clothe himself in a more benevolent or paternalistic garb. It would seem, then, that what is required is business statesmanship.

Over thirty years ago, a theory of corporate social responsibility called the managerial creed[2] was proposed as a position that is replacing the older classical view, i.e., business has no social responsibilities other than to produce goods and services efficiently, make money for shareholders, and conduct business in a lawful manner.[3] The managerial creed maintains that managerial responsibility pertains to the basic constituencies that are affected by the actions of the corporation and not merely to shareholders. Managers should balance the legitimate, though often competing, claims of shareholders, customers, employees, suppliers, and the general public in a just or fair manner. This view is Platonic in that the emphasis is on both a grasp of the whole and on managerial ethics. Since Plato would probably view business statesmanship as analogous to political statesmanship, he would argue that it requires knowledge necessary for guiding an organized whole and both sound moral and economic leadership.

As applied to modern corporate business, the managerial creed is morally sounder than the classical view.[4] Modern business is too large to be a purely economic institution; it is not self-regulating for the greater good, and it affects too many people. From the standpoint of justice, it must act as a social as well as an economic institution. Insofar as the corporate executive perceives business to be a purely economic institution, he will continue to incur the hostility of people and perpetuate the image of business as an amoral, or even an immoral, institution.

E. F. Schumacher saw clearly how reducing all business problems to those of economics greatly simplifies the operations of business.[5] Bottom line problems are much easier to solve than ethical, or more generally qualitative, problems. Business statesmanship, therefore, requires an attitude, as well as an education, quite different from that which is typical of the traditional business executive. But the modern business executive, because of his emphasis on finance, is often quite resistant to an orientation that would be more productive of business statesmanship. Thus, his talk about a "managerial creed" is often viewed as a manipulative device of management.[6] The corporation is often perceived as having little time or inclination to dwell on the needs of the consumer or, in certain respects, on those of the employee when not viewed from the standpoint of increased productivity. The doctrine of corporate social responsibility, in this context, tends to look like lip service, and the capacity of corporate business to reduce doubts about their sense of social responsibility by creating images that counter these doubts do not seem to be doing them much good.[7]

Businesspeople have been critical of universities, particularly liberal arts colleges, for helping to perpetuate a public dislike of business. In Chapter 2, I attempted to show that business's distrust of the liberal arts is rooted in an anti-intellectualism that has been nurtured by American business traditions. In spite of the businessperson's distrust of the liberal arts, it is such an education that is necessary to supplement the more vocationally-oriented business curriculum in order to gain greater ethical sensitivity or knowledge and that wider perspective necessary for business statesmanship.[8]

Some interesting work has been done recently on the relation between liberal arts education and business, e.g., by the Corporate Council on the Liberal Arts. Certain skills have been touted in emphasizing the importance of liberal arts education for corporate leadership—e.g., communication skills, interpersonal and problem solving skills, critical and analytical skills. Helpful attitudes that liberal arts education can bring to business have also been discussed—e.g., tolerance for ambiguity, complexity, and change; lack of dogmatism and prejudice; curiosity, and a love of learning. But as important as these skills and attitudes are for corporate leadership, liberal arts education is most essential for business statesmanship or leadership, as I have suggested, for it helps to develop conceptual and synthetic skills—skills necessary to grasp the presuppositions and principles underlying a whole—as well as a humane business character.

The search for comprehensive and interdisciplinary truths, the original goal of philosophy, is undermined by an overemphasis on specialization. Liberal arts education, if it is truly liberal, must avoid this twentieth century emphasis. It can do this by returning to the spirit of ancient Greek education (*paideia*). *Paideia* entails the cultivation of the whole person, the development of a person's capacities or abilities; in this way, one can best respond to the challenges of life and live a happy life (*eudaimonia*). This view should be contrasted with a conception of education which makes technical or vocational instruction central.[9] If education is reduced to specialized training, the emphasis on technology and instrumental values would influence people to emphasize immediate practical concerns; technology would become people's master rather than slave, and instrumental values would be elevated to the status of intrinsic values. To the ancient Greek thinker, e.g., Plato or Aristotle, such a position, by limiting the development of both the human intellect and character, creates a myopic view of life which makes one incapable of examining basic human values and thus living the good life.

Drucker, in a recent book, says that management is a liberal art; it "deals with people, their values, their growth and development."[10] Thus, Drucker supports the view of ancient Greek *paideia*. In developing this, he emphasizes both the comprehensive and interdisciplinary nature of management.

> Management is...what tradition used to call a liberal art—'lib-
> eral' because it deals with the fundamentals of knowledge,
> self-knowledge, wisdom and leadership; 'art' because it is
> practice and application. Managers draw on all the knowledges
> and insights of the humanities and the social sciences—on
> psychology and philosophy, on economics and history, on the
> physical sciences and ethics.[11]

If we take the view of the ancient Greek philosophers (Plato and Aristotle) and attempt to understand the values that properly determine life as a whole, we must be open to these values; it is not enough to be a generalist in the sense of being a jack-of-all-intellectual-trades. There is a difference between being a lover of wisdom and a dilettante. In order to be open to proper values, we must understand the human soul and its education. According to the above thinkers, this entails reflection on excellence (*aretē*), viz., excellence of character and intellectual excellence. Moreover, it is the intrinsic, rather than instrumental, value of virtue that requires emphasis. The liberal person is the free person and, therefore, is not a slave to the body or possessions. Distractions and entertainment used to service the body parody a proper life of leisure, and the overemphasis on work or career as having merely instrumental value parody a just society. The dual danger is the lack of appreciation of the intrinsic value of one's work, and the overemphasis on the values of a bogus (trivial) life of leisure.

2. Plato on the Human Soul and the Cardinal Virtues

It is no wonder that a liberal arts orientation is often viewed as diametrically opposed to the values and practices of business. In the sections which follow this one, I shall attempt to show that from a Platonic point of view (one which I believe has great merit) the values of many businesspeople are destructive to each aspect of the human soul and, therefore, basically distort a proper perspective on virtue. Since an understanding of this part of the chapter requires some knowledge of Plato's analysis of the human soul and his related conception of the ancient Greek cardinal virtues, knowledge which the reader may not possess, in this section, I shall summarize Plato's view of these concepts.

In the *Republic*, Plato constructs a supposedly ideal city. Being completely good, it is said to contain the four cardinal or principal virtues—wisdom, courage, temperance, and justice. Since the virtues that exist in the city are derived from the character of its citizens, the cardinal virtues are applicable to them. These virtues, however, can only be understood in relation to the elements and the proper relationship among the elements of the human soul. In the *Republic*, Plato analyzes the human soul into three elements. The highest is reason which has a drive (*hormē*) for the truth or knowledge, and a desire to govern the entire soul.[12] The next highest element is called spirit. It is most clearly manifested in anger and is the competitive, ambitious, aggressive, contentious aspect of the soul.[13] Honor is its highest goal, but it often will settle for victory.[14] The lowest element of the human soul is appetite. Appetites include both physical desires for food, drink, sex, and material appetites for money and possessions.[15]

Having analyzed the three elements of the human soul, Plato is then able to define the four cardinal virtues in terms of the proper functions of the soul's elements and the proper relationships that should exist among these elements. A wise person is rational in the highest sense. Plato identifies such a person with the philosopher who most completely embodies the two primary purposes of reason—to gain knowledge of the good for organized wholes (individuals, cities, and the cosmos), and to govern the soul properly for the benefit of the entire soul. The philosopher, then, should be the ruler (king) of the good city. He or she provides the good counsel that is basic to political wisdom or statesmanship. Unlike specialized forms of knowledge necessary to the city, wisdom entails knowledge of the good for the city as a whole.[16]

In the courageous person, spirit is the ally of reason[17] (a consequence of proper character education); it takes reason's lead concerning what is and is not to be feared (dangerous), and it tenaciously adheres to reason's right opinions. Those citizens in whom the spirited element is dominant become the Auxiliaries (soldiers) of the city. (Spirit, properly trained, is reason's helper.) They are said to be the repository of the city's courage, but their raw courage or spiritedness is nurtured by right opinion (concerning what is and is not to be feared) derived from the philosopher-kings; the courage of the philosopher-kings, therefore, appears to be of a higher order. Nonetheless, the courage of the Auxiliaries provides necessary support for the pronouncements of the rulers. The stability of this support is grounded in the character of the Auxiliaries which protects them from acting against their principles in spite of the seductiveness of pleasure (the lure of the objects of desire), and the fears inspired by the possibility of pain and death.

The remaining two virtues, temperance and justice, are determined by relationships among the elements of the soul in the individual and among the classes in the city. In the soul of the temperate person, according to Plato, there is an agreement between reason (the natural ruler) and spirit and appetite (the natural subjects) as to what ought to rule and what ought to be ruled.[18] It is no wonder, then, that Plato determines temperance in the city to be an agreement between rulers and those who are ruled as to who ought to rule.[19]

In the *Republic*, there are two classes subject to the rule of philosopher-kings, the Auxiliaries and a third class which performs the economic functions of the city. Finally, justice in the individual is described as the virtue that ensures psychic harmony and integrity;[20] it is *par excellence* the virtue of the whole—whether it be an individual, a city, the cosmos or, in our case, the corporation. Justice in the individual is defined as each element of the soul doing the work nature assigns to it,[21] and in the city, justice obtains when each of the three classes performs its own "job," not interfering with the functions of the other classes.[22] Justice implies that each part of the whole should be properly situated relative to the other parts of the whole; in this way, the good of the whole is achieved, i.e., the basic needs of the constituents of the whole are fulfilled, while the whole, itself, is healthy or functions well.

3. Business Values and the Appetites

A popular view of corporate business is that the goal of big business is profit maximization. The history of traditional American business values, according to my analysis, emphasizes materialistic values. On this view, business must continually cater to and stimulate bodily appetites. This, according to Plato, is totally contrary to the good of the human soul. The appetites are governed by the principle of physical pleasure and the avoidance of pain; they are resistant to rational guidance and are prone to excess. Appetites, as we saw, include both physical desires for food, drink, sex, and materialistic appetites for money and possessions. According to Plato, what is best for the human soul is the nurturing or "educating" of human appetites to accord with that which is rational by habituating them to be pleased by the intrinsically good and pained by the intrinsically bad. He would, then, consider business leadership of the above type to be tyranny or the perversion of statesmanship. Statesmen attempt to habituate the human soul to virtue; catering to the appetites, on the other hand, perverts each of the cardinal virtues—wisdom, temperance, justice and courage.

The tendency to intemperance produced by indulging the appetites is patent. Callicles, in Plato's *Gorgias*, maintains that the person who lives as he ought to—one who is wise, courageous, and naturally just—is best at expanding his appetites and satisfying them by catering to each of them. The denial of this is a rationalization for one's cowardice and general inability to satisfy all of our desires. Socrates admits that Callicles has uncovered a real hypocrisy in people's view of virtue, but Callicles's intemperate person is much like an addict. His soul is like a leaky jar which he is constantly attempting to fill in order to escape pain. The more one gets, the more one wants and thus one becomes insatiable.[23] The happy life cannot reasonably be equated with the insatiable one or, to change the image, one in which our life is devoted to scratching an endless itch.[24]

Galbraith applies the Platonic position to big business. Corporations want people to believe that the consumer is sovereign; that, in a primary sense, it is the consumer who basically influences the producer. Since greater affluence, the ability to consume more, is thought to lead to greater happiness, the happy person, as Callicles says, is expert at expanding his appetites while being able to satisfy them all. Therefore, big business can propagate the belief that increased productivity or growth is a most worthy social goal as an axiom, for it makes for the possibility of happiness. In reality, as Plato suggests in the Allegory of the Cave, Callicles's happy person is a creation of sophistry. In Galbraith's terms, man as consumer is not sovereign; he is rather the creation of a vast organized network that controls demand by creating so-called needs which, in reality, are puffed-up wants. Callicles's happy person is deluded into thinking that his wants are freely determined by himself; they are really manipulated by big business for the purpose of increased productivity. The consumer is made to feel that he needs more and more things because he is made to think that increased consumption is identical with increased happiness. Just as Plato suggests that Callicles's happy person is a slave rather than a master, so Galbraith maintains that man as consumer is "bamboozled" by big business into believing that he is a type of sovereign when, in reality, he is made dependent upon puffed-up wants as felt needs. Therefore, consumer "bamboozlement" not only confuses freedom with slavery, it distorts our perspective by confusing real and illusory needs. Galbraith suggests that the sophistry of big business convinces people that they are basically deprived of what they really need if they do not consume what big business produces.[25] In Platonic terms, business creates feelings of deprivation, and strong feelings of pain (deprivation) create an overestimation of the value of that which alleviates the pain.[26] The pleasures of the consumeristic life, and the consequent overestimation of the value of materialism, may well be projections based upon the negations of our feelings of deprivation and, therefore, distortions of a proper value perspective.

It is not an accident, then, that for the ancient Greek, "*sōphrosunē*" not only meant temperance but also a type of practical wisdom or soundness of mind. Consumer addiction and the confusion of real with apparent needs certainly do undermine practical wisdom. In the *Phaedo*, Plato suggests that the body is a singular distraction to the discovery of truth. "The body intrudes...into our investigations, interrupting, disturbing, distracting, and preventing us from getting a glimpse of the truth."[27]

Daniel Bell maintains that when capitalism was severed from the restraints of the Protestant ethic, its cultural and moral justification became hedonism.[28] He correctly argues that this view is a reversal of the Platonic hierarchy of human capacities.[29] He also correctly maintains that the change from Protestant asceticism to hedonism parallels Plato's discussion of the change from the healthy to the fevered city.[30] He thinks that this change in values is the basis of a contradiction in modern business. He argues that corporate business expects temperate, disciplined behavior from employees; that is, they should work hard, diligently pursue their careers, and accept delayed gratification. On the other hand, "in its products and its advertisements, the corporation promotes pleasure, instant joy, relaxation and letting go."[31] Thus, a Protestant ethic is demanded of people as producers and a materialistic hedonism as a consumer.[32]

Emphasis on the physical appetites, or physical pleasure and the avoidance of pain, places a premium on acquisitiveness and on that which is easy, comfortable, secure, and stable. But if we consider common varieties of injustice—cheating, stealing, and lying—the possible advantages of such conduct, assuming that one can get away with injustice, are materialistic and broadly based upon the pursuit of pleasure and the avoidance of pain. Moreover, the tendency to intemperance, stimulated by an overemphasis on the importance of the body and material things, encourages injustice.

Our final concern, in this section, is to argue that catering to our appetites undermines courage, in a proper sense of the term. We saw that, in the *Republic*, Plato defines the courage of the Auxiliaries as a character trait that entails adherence to principles determined by right opinions about what is and what is not to be feared (dangerous); these right opinions are based upon accepting the authority of the philosopher-kings. Maccoby, in *The Gamesman*, captures a substantial part of the meaning of Platonic courage when he distinguishes between "guts" and "courage."[33] The gutsy person has a strong appetite for certain goals and will take risks to achieve them, but guts can be displayed without concern for moral principles, and without a commitment to principles central to the self (courage entails integrity). Courage cannot be separated from integrity or, in general, from morality. Plato, however, goes further than Maccoby; he insists that the highest type of courage entails knowledge of what is and what is not dangerous, and this implies knowledge of proper values.

Spiritedness, the natural basis for courage—which is related to such traits as energy (drive), assertiveness, boldness, self-confidence, innovativeness, and especially, competitiveness and ambition—can be directed toward what is noble or fine (*kalon*) or toward the attainment of the objects of appetite. From a Platonic point of view, some businesspeople make the mistake of reducing the objects of spiritedness to the economic factors in life. At times, they give the impression that the only type of "real" competitiveness is that which is exhibited in the pursuit of wealth and power. In this context, Plato's spirited Auxiliaries would be changed from well-bred watch dogs to wolves.[34] In describing the degeneration of the Platonic Auxiliary into, first, the timocratic and, then, the oligarchic person, Plato maintains that the concern for wealth and property causes the spirited person to separate spiritedness from the "noble" principles that reason dictates. In this way, spiritedness becomes a servant of materialistic ambition. Ambition readily degenerates into avarice. The clever, ambitious person makes wealth the measure of all value, and intelligence and ambition are myopically directed to this end. The American robber barons of the late 19th and early 20th centuries are models of this degenerative form of spiritedness.

Although materialistic motivations can, as we have seen, stimulate a type of conventional courage in the form of entrepreneurial risktaking, for a number of people materialism has quite a different effect. For many people (and clearly for the conventional materialist), the avoidance of pain is a greater motivator than the pursuit of pleasure. A life that is easy, comfortable, safe, and secure is clearly a dominant goal for people we ordinarily describe as materialistic. If this is the case, it is easy to see how being dominated by a materialistic value system tends to erode courage.

We saw that the business character type that best fits the above description is Whyte's organization man. He is quite similar to Plato's oligarchic man who is conventionally moral and, consequently, motivated by fear of punishment and concern for rewards rather than moral conviction. He is considered respectable, but his morality is superficial rather than real. He is neither competitive nor ambitious for fear of losing his wealth; in consequence, his courage is eroded.[35]

4. Business Values and Spiritedness

I have briefly considered spiritedness with reference to courage and, generally, as a servant of materialistic desires. But, as is suggested in Chapter 4, more can be said concerning the dangers of certain business values for the spirited person.

In the *Republic*, Plato mentions the aggressiveness inherent in the nature of the spirited person. It is necessary to temper such a person's aggressiveness so that he will be courageous when this virtue is called for, but also gentle when such a quality is necessary.[36] His energy and initiative may tend to make him too tough and uncouth or an unintelligent philistine. On the other hand, a temperament that is too gentle is excessively soft. The proper mixture of both temperaments will help to nurture a humane, intelligent person.[37] We saw that, in the *Statesman*, Plato develops this theme in more detail. When the traits of either the courageous or temperate character types are taken to extremes and embodied in leaders, destruction to organized wholes (e.g., cities) is the result. The passion for peaceloving traits creates a person of soft character whose cowardice and sluggishness make him incapable of responding to the challenges of life, while the passion for the warlike traits produces a person who is excessively aggressive, competitive, and violent; in either case, the results are devastation and destruction. It is clear from what was said in Chapter 4 that an excess of spiritedness in the robber baron character type and a deficiency of spiritedness in the organization man type are both destructive, and a weaving of beneficial traits from both types is necessary to develop spiritedness properly in leaders.

Since Plato's position, with reference to the history of American business values, was developed in some detail in the preceding chapter, we need not belabor the point that certain American business values have undermined spiritedness with reference to *all* the ancient Greek cardinal virtues. We have seen the tendency in American business values either to reduce courage to excessive competitiveness, human bestiality, and unbridled materialistic ambition or, in the case of organization man values, to reduce courage to cowardice and a lack of integrity. Temperance clearly applies, as Plato thought, to spirit as well as to the appetites. We have seen how pre and postdepression American business values led to an intemperate individualism, in the former case, and an intemperate lack of individualism in the latter case. The temperate or mean position between extremes, in both cases, was avoided. Because of this, human spiritedness was separated from Plato's "divine bond" which is the basis of the statesman's (practical) wisdom. Finally, we have seen that it is not only extreme American business individualism that has created injustices in society, excessive organization man values have the same effect.

5. Business Values and Reason

Plato argues that decisions are often made, not by thinking about the good of the entire soul, but because certain appetites happen to be strong or because of the strength of certain emotions, e.g., the anger of the spirited person. When reason functions in the service of one's appetites and emotions, reason attempts to determine adequate means for achieving the ends posited by them. Since the entire soul is not attended to—i.e., reason, in this sense, is not considering human action from the standpoint of what is good for the entire soul (what Plato calls justice)—some human needs must be frustrated, because certain human capacities will be unfulfilled. The primary function of reason is to make statesmanlike judgments about the good for the entire soul, and this depends upon gaining the broad perspective necessary to understand what the human goods are.[38] This function of reason is essential to manage in accordance with the managerial creed. Justice can only be served if the needs of all of our capacities are given their "due" or are "managed" so as to produce the greatest amount of good (for the soul) possible. Reason, in this sense, provides the guiding principle for properly implementing the managerial creed. To achieve the above purpose of reason, reason's own peculiar drive (*hormē*), the desire for the truth or knowledge, is indispensable.

Both the statesman-like function of reason and its peculiar drive to discover the truth or to seek knowledge have been undermined by some of the values and practices of American business. Indeed, the argument has returned to points made at the beginning of the chapter.

If the leaders of corporate business believe that big business is fundamentally an economic rather than a quasi-social and political institution—and this still appears to be the view of most business leaders[39]—then business statesmanship, in the Platonic sense, will be forsaken. As we have seen, business's narrow emphasis on economic concerns and the tendency to simplify business operations by appealing primarily to such concerns undermine a legitimate notion of corporate social responsibility.

However, we have seen that, in addition to the above difficulty, the Platonic conception of (corporate) statesmanship must face the stubbornness of an antiliberal arts, and at times anti-intellectual, American business tradition. Leonard Silk and David Vogel recall the familiar remark of some businesspeople, "If you're so smart, why ain't you rich?"[40] We saw that the predepression American business ethic nurtured this antiliberal arts emphasis in business. From the perspective of the Protestant ethic (especially as applied to the later Puritan merchants), cultural and liberal arts pursuits tend to be decadent, and the leisure necessary to cultivate oneself is identified with idleness and wastefulness. The frontier and robber baron ethics emphasized a narrowly practical view of human intelligence, one which is incompatible with an appreciation of a liberal arts education. But dominant postdepression business values, such as those of the organization man, did nothing to moderate this position.

I suggested in Chapter 1 that this bias towards economic considerations and against broad-based intellectual concerns is manifested in the reduction of the distinctly rational drive for knowledge (or the truth) to a desire for determining values that are instrumental rather than intrinsic. The passion for knowledge, when allied with broad intellectual concerns, as Plato suggests, is directed toward gaining knowledge of intrinsic values. This is not the attitude of the traditional American businessperson who assumes that our basic values are economic and, therefore, we should develop virtues that best serve economic goals. We saw that the frontier ethic, inherited by the robber barons, stresses, according to Turner, the ability to find the expedient way to solve the practical problems of life, i.e., yankee know-how, can do, or having smarts.[41] No wonder there is so much fascination with technology that its dangers are often overlooked. There is little that business has done to change this bias substantially. It has been slow to recognize the intrinsic value of work, or of quality products, or most important, the intrinsic value of people.

There is a third danger that is related to the traditional businessperson's view of the human intellect. According to this view, rational objectivity does not seem to be valued very highly. We have seen that traditional American business emphasizes the competitive spirit and its objects—survival and, most of all, winning. The human intellect becomes the means *par excellence* of manipulating people and things to serve these ends. This attitude makes it impossible to reflect honestly about human values so that one can understand legitimate criticisms and modify one's values accordingly. One of Plato's major criticisms of the Sophists is that they lacked concern for objectivity and, consequently, emphasized winning rather than determining the truth.

The problem of rational objectivity with respect to the traditional businessperson can be further illuminated in the context of the weaving analogy in the *Statesman*. The spirited element which is the natural ingredient in courage is essential for business statesmen. As innovative and creative thinkers, they must be daring enough to see things from new or fresh perspectives, and courageous enough to put up with the Socratic type of insecurity that comes from questioning conventional wisdom. But it is not possible to make fair or unbiased judgments about values without Socratic humility, nor are such judgments possible if we do not have the daring to pursue unconventional ideas or lines of inquiry. Therefore, the overly temperate character of the organization man must be avoided. But a managerial statesman must also be temperate or modest in order to control intellectual *hybris*. As much as he or she needs such spirited qualities as assertiveness or initiative, daring or boldness, a drive to take risks in spite of one's desire for safety and security, excessive "courageous" traits destroy one's sense of fairness. Such a person will never give his opponent his due and, therefore, will not consider points of view different from his own. Moreover, by being excessively competitive, he will tend to view the goal of any argument as winning rather than the truth. Instead of viewing rational discussion as a cooperative enterprise among friends trying to reach the truth, it becomes a competitive battle in which anything goes in order to achieve victory. Thus, the overly courageous character of the robber baron must also be avoided.

The above antiPlatonic position concerning the human intellect and values can readily be seen to have the most disastrous effects on human virtue. Wisdom in the Platonic sense is clearly undermined, and since spiritedness is not guided by wisdom, it degenerates, as we have seen, into a bogus form of courage. Since the function of reason is reduced to determining the means to economic ends, it readily functions as a servant rather than a master of human appetites (encouraging intemperance), and since it does not reflect on the intrinsic values related to the whole, it will not effectively "temper" the excesses of spiritedness. Finally, as Plato says, if reason does not reflect on the whole, the legitimate needs of each of the parts will not be met, and injustice will be the result. In our context, corporate leaders will rationalize (in the pejorative sense) injustices to employees, consumers, not to mention society in general. In conclusion, if businesspeople refuse to consider the ethical, social, and quasi-political functions of big business (if they refuse to understand business in a broader sense than that which is typical), and if they limit the powers of reason to determining instrumental values and to manipulating whatever is necessary in order to survive and achieve "victory," human virtue in the classical sense would be destroyed.

I shall illustrate this position by considering a contemporary business writer. Albert Z. Carr mentions the following qualities ("virtues") he considers basic for promotion because they, supposedly, benefit a company at its higher levels: the ability to get along with and work well with others and undermine antagonisms, decisiveness and gutsiness, poise and staying under control, and creating "good ideas."[42] These qualities bear some resemblance to justice, courage, temperance, and wisdom. As one develops these so-called virtues, they serve as "strategic principles" for personal success.[43] In themselves, the above qualities serve a purpose, but as expressions of the cardinal virtues, they are so narrow, or Machiavellian, that they pervert the higher good for both the individual and the organization. Carr admits that the "virtues" he considers are strictly instrumental for success—wealth, power, prestige, and security. He admits that the business-person who espouses such putative virtues is not a professional. They are therefore incompatible with justice in a proper sense. Carr's wisdom is a clear example of the reduction of wisdom to cleverness described by Aristotle.

A wiser position is taken by Schumacher in *Small is Beautiful*. The cardinal virtues are said to be basic to solving modern problems. He correctly says that a prudent (practically wise) attitude is not "a small, mean, calculating attitude to life."[44] Practical wisdom is the "mother" of the virtues because it entails a grasp of the whole—what Schumacher calls "reality." He concludes his book by saying:

> Only on the basis of this magnanimous kind of prudence can we achieve justice, fortitude, and *temperantia*…. The type of realism which behaves as if the good, the true, and the beautiful were too vague and subjective to be adopted as the highest aims of social or individual life, or were the automatic spin-off of the successful pursuit of wealth and power, has been aptly called 'crackpot-realism.' Everywhere people ask: 'What can I actually *do*?' The answer is as simple as it is disconcerting: we can, each of us, work to put our own inner house in order [Platonic justice]. The guidance we need for this work cannot be found in science or technology, the value of which utterly depends on the ends they serve; but it can still be found in the traditional wisdom of mankind [the cardinal virtues].[45]

NOTES

1. Howard J. Laski, *The American Democracy, A Commentary and an Interpretation* (New York: Viking Press, 1948), p. 165.

2. Francis X. Sutton, Seymour E. Harris, Carl Haysen, and James Toben, *The American Business Creed* (Cambridge: Harvard University Press, 1956).

3. Milton Friedman, "The Social Responsibility of Business is to Increase Its Profits," *New York Times Magazine* (Sept. 13 1970).

4. The classical view is based upon laissez-faire theory, but this theory was never intended to apply to a business world dominated by large corporations and, generally, by oligopoly rather than pluralism.

5. E. F. Schumacher, *Small is Beautiful: Economics as if People Mattered* (New York: Perennial Library, 1973), pp. 44–46.

6. While presenting the image of a well-intentioned manager, one could justify, for example, not giving employees a raise by maintaining that the raise would have to be passed on to the consumer or would be contrary to the interests of the shareholders who would not accept it. Generally, each group could be manipulated with arguments of this sort, one group being played off against another.

7. The following is possibly a more realistic, and certainly a more pessimistic, picture of how a managerial creed would work. Different groups affected by corporate decisions will exert different, and often incompatible, pressures on management. Unions want higher wages, etc., shareholders want higher dividends, consumers want lower prices. In practice, might makes right; that is, management will yield in proportion to the greater force.

8. Alfred N. Whitehead argues that managers require a quality he calls foresight. Foresight as to the necessary changes that may have to be made in a corporation is based upon the habit of understanding basic principles—those which pertain to the outside environment and its values as well as those which apply to the internal workings of the corporation. Alfred N. Whitehead, *Adventures in Ideas* (New York: Mentor Book, 1955), Chapt. 6.

9. Plato and Aristotle refused to distinguish sharply between ethical and nonethical realms of activity. One should be fundamentally concerned with the excellence of the whole of one's life, of which one's career is a part. Human excellences or

virtues should be manifest in our lives and not merely in circumscribed parts of our lives. One important consequence of this is the benefit of the virtuous person to society. His or her generosity is not a part of one's life, e.g., the occasional gift giver or philanthropist, it is a consequence of living the good life.

10. Peter F. Drucker, *The New Realities* (New York: Harper and Row, 1989), p. 231.

11. Drucker, p. 231.

12. *Republic* 474c–475c, 581b, 441e, 442c.

13. *Republic* 357a–b, 441a–b, 442b–c; *Statesman* 311b.

14. *Republic* 439e, 581a–b; *Phaedrus* 253d.

15. *Republic* 441b–c, 442b, 439c–d, 436a, 580d–581a; *Phaedrus* 237d; *Laws* 875c; *Timaeus* 34c, 69d.

16. *Republic* 428b–d.

17. *Republic* 440b–d.

18. *Republic* 442c–d.

19. *Republic* 431d–432a.

20. *Republic* 443d.

21. *Republic* 441e–442d, 443c–444b.

22. *Republic* 433a–434c.

23. *Gorgias* 491e–494a.

24. *Gorgias* 494c. Similarly, in the *Republic*, the tyrant who thinks he is a free man and master is, in reality, a slave to insatiable desires (*Republic* 578a–b).

25. John. K. Galbraith, *The New Industrial State* (New York: Signet Books, 1967), Chapt. XVIII, pp. 221–222, 302. Cf. John K. Galbraith, *The Affluent Society* (New York: Mentor Book, 1958), Chapt. XI.

26. See, for example, *Philebus* 41e–42c; *Republic* 583d–584a, 584e–585a.

27. *Phaedo* 66d; cf. *Philebus* 250c, *Republic* 485c–e.

28. Daniel Bell, *The Cultural Contradictions of Capitalism* (New York: Basic Books, 1976), pp. 21–22.

29. Bell, p. 22.

30. Bell, p. 82.

31. Bell, pp. 71–72.

32. Bell, p. 75.

33. Michael Maccoby, *The New Corporate Leaders: The Gamesman* (New York: Simon and Schuster, 1976), pp. 181–182.

34. *Republic* 416–417b.

35. *Republic* 554c–555a.

36. *Republic* 375a–d.

37. *Republic* 410d–411e.

38. Plato describes this broad-based knowledge as knowledge of absolute beauty in the *Symposium* (211e–212a), and of the good in the *Republic* (505a, 519). The philosopher, says Plato, "is the spectator of all time and existence" (*Republic* 486a).

39. As Leonard Silk and David Vogel say [*Ethics and Profits: The Crisis of Confidence in American Business* (New York: Simon and Schuster, 1976)], for most businessmen, "the world is seen essentially as a marketplace, and the overriding objective of virtually everyone is considered to be personal gain." This is their own perspective which they project onto the world (p. 209; cf. pp. 112, 233).

40. Silk and Vogel, *Ethics and Profits*, p. 122.

41. Alan Trachtenburg says, "By the 1850's, the practical Yankee inventor-entrepreneur, the tinkerer with an eye on profit, had come to seem an American type." *The Incorporation of America: Culture and Society in the Gilded Age* (New York: Hill and Wang, 1982), p. 54.

42. Albert Z. Carr, *Business as a Game* (New York: Mentor Book, 1968), p. 89.

43. One can see how Carr develops this, for example, on p. 112.

44. Schumacher, p. 296.

45. Schumacher, p. 297.

CHAPTER VI

BUSINESS IN A PLATONIC MOLD

I have argued that a Platonic business organization is one in which managerial statesmen provide the leadership. Justice will be based upon management in accordance with a proper managerial creed, e.g., employees will develop their abilities relative to their careers while contributing to the good of the firm, consumers will get quality goods and services, shareholders will do well. As far as virtue is concerned, the ancient Greek cardinal virtues will be in evidence in a Platonic form. This chapter will be devoted to showing one way in which a Platonic type of business organization is possible. I shall begin by looking for the source of such an organization in the managerial philosophy of the following members of the Stanford School— Richard T. Pascale, Anthony G. Athos, William G. Ouchi, and Peters and Waterman.

1. The Stanford School and Platonic Business Leadership

For Plato (and Aristotle as well), epistemological metholology is based upon whether the subject matter we are considering is changeable or permanent. This is basic to Plato's distinction between the realms of opinion and knowledge in the *Republic*. It is also fundamental to the distinction between *phronēsis* (practical wisdom) and *sophia* (theoretical wisdom), in the *Nicomachean Ethics*, for Aristotle. Business phenomena are notoriously changeable and, therefore, proper business leadership entails a wisdom which is different from that which is required by mathematics and the physical sciences; it must be more flexible. Thus, Peters and Waterman are correct when they argue that an excellent company must be defined as one which changes when the environment changes. The traditional American business ethic which emphasizes courageous character traits is essential to counterbalance the much more temperate character traits manifested in modern business which tend to stultify corporate change or flexibility, not to mention undermine corporate character.

Pascale correctly argues that we should seek a middle ground between extreme individuality and extreme conformity,[1] but he does not show how this can be done. He merely mentions, as a fact, that certain firms with strong cultures which mold (socialize) employees to fit their cultures do encourage healthy competition and do not lose innovativeness. In *The Art of Japanese Management*,[2] Pascale and Athos argue that because the Japanese value system emphasizes interdependence (the parts of some whole are mutually dependent), rather than independence, which the western value system supports, the Japanese have a cultural advantage in business. This may be the case, given the nature of the modern corporation, but if the Japanese position breeds organization men, may we not argue that this advantage can easily turn into a disadvantage for business?

Ouchi, in *Theory Z*,[3] does raise the question of whether or not an imitation of Japanese collectivism by western firms creates organization men—in his terms, a paternalistic context in which workers want to belong to some larger whole which will take care of them and control their lives. Unfortunately, he too merely states what he considers to be the facts without coping with the problem. He maintains that such firms are just as aggressive and independent-minded as typical American firms. He does admit, however, that some Japanese-type firms can be paternalistic to the point of becoming "smothering and all-encompassing." There is one point he mentions, vague though it be, which is helpful. The Japanese-type culture, according to Ouchi, offers employees a stable environment from which support can be gained to cope with their problems, but there is also a great deal of autonomy exhibited by such firms. He does elaborate somewhat by suggesting that an egalitarian, rather than authoritarian, attitude permeates these firms, and this, according to Ouchi, entails that each person can work autonomously without close supervision, relying on his or her own judgment. This approach, which attempts to mix adequately a concern for stability or security with an emphasis on autonomy, is developed, as we shall soon see, by Peters and Waterman.

If Plato is correct and his model in the *Statesman* is to be followed, corporate founding fathers or models of corporate leadership (corporate statesmen) must ground their leadership on an understanding of the real corporate goods. Such wisdom will guide a proper weaving of the conflicting character traits in those people who have leadership positions in the corporation.[4]

Peters and Waterman (in *In Search of Excellence*) criticize big business for overemphasizing finance, quantitative analysis, and generally, short term, bottom line concerns. They maintain that short-term tactics and strategies do not make for successful companies. In contrast to this traditional business approach, the Stanford School argues that successful firms are fundamentally based upon a system of shared values; these values inspire employees to dedicate themselves to goals "beyond profit" (Pascale and Athos)[5] or to "beautiful" goals (Peters and Waterman).[6] Such dedication is basic to productive performance. Peters and Waterman maintain that the shared values of "excellent" firms is their essential quality, and Pascale and Athos argue that "the bond of shared values" is the "secret weapon" of successful firms.[7] Both sets of authors emphasize that the shared values provide a "larger meaning" or purpose for employees, one which promises them dignity. Evidently these shared values pertain to corporate managers (leaders) as well as to corporate employees. Ouchi also emphasizes the notion that success in business depends upon formulating an adequate corporate culture based upon shared values, and this culture must reflect unselfish cooperative attitudes rather than merely bottom line concerns. Such a conception is closer to organizational values that are true goods (Plato's "divine bond") than is the more typically bottom line value concerns of corporations. However, the Stanford School must, still, provide a clearer analysis of the values of a successful corporate culture; what, then, are its "beautiful" values?

According to Peters and Waterman (*In Search of Excellence*), these firms emphasize quality and reliable products and services and concern for people. These values are related, for they correctly argue that personal satisfaction and pride in one's accomplishments can be based upon producing quality and reliable goods and services. Thus, such management is concerned with its employees in a way that is fundamental to the individual. In general, excellent companies create environments in which employees can develop their abilities and be treated with respect and dignity. Therefore, they take pride in the firm and the firm benefits from the skills of the employees.

If business modifies its values and practices along the lines suggested by Peters and Waterman, the Platonic criticism of business developed in Chapters 4 and 5 will have to be substantially moderated. The model of the just citizen in the *Republic* is the dedicated craftsman, especially when we consider craftsmanship in a broad generic sense. Peters and Waterman's conception of "beautiful" corporate values is essentially a craftsmanship model. Therefore, I should elaborate on the notion of craftsmanship and the ideal of a managerial craftsman.[8]

Excellence, i.e., quality and reliable products and service, and a concern for people, as I have said, are the bases of proper corporate values according to Peters and Waterman. With reference to, at least, the former characteristic, it would seem that the character model that ought to be emphasized for both management and employees in general is a craftsmanship model. The goal of craftsmanship is to create that which has quality or excellence; personal satisfaction, pride in accomplishment, and a sense of dignity derived from the concern for self-development are the motivations. For want of a better term, I call this the generic concept of craftsmanship. A business management craftsman attempts to create a quality organization and quality products and services as a result of such an organization.[9] Such excellence ought to be, as Peters and Waterman suggest, the keynote for an organization's orientation toward people and, therefore, entails their second basic constituent of the "divine bond"—a concern for people.

We have seen that, in the Platonic state, the just citizen does his own business, i.e., sticks to what he does best. In consequence, justice creates a proper harmony (integrity) in the city; each person is able to fulfill basic capacities, with some compromises, while contributing in essential ways to the common good. In an "excellent" company, it is the ideal of the just citizen that should filter through the firm, and management should provide the moral example of such an ideal; that is, as I have said, a business management craftsman attempts to create a quality organization, and quality products and services are the result of such an organization. Thomas Watson of IBM is an example of such a managerial craftsman. Like any good statesman, he thought about the basic values that should guide his organization and emphasized those which truly have intrinsic worth. Above all, having concern for his workers, he encouraged them to develop their abilities; this, he believed, would help them to enjoy and take pride in their work. It would also help them to take pride in the firm. Thus, the interests of the workers would coincide with those of the firm (this is essential to Platonic justice).

Watson's beliefs accord with Plato's notion of political statesmanship which, as we saw, requires a knowledge of those values that make an organized whole good.[10] Such statesmanship embodies practical wisdom. A firm guided by such wisdom will, of course, produce quality products and services. It was Watson who invented what the Japanese call "continuous learning"—continual training sessions which help one to improve that which is already done well. Clearly, under such guidance, spirited management will be properly directed by managerial wisdom so that robber baron (or jungle fighter) and even gamesman tendencies, with the consequent human manipulation and overemphasis on winning, would not be allowed to develop. The organization man mentality would be undermined by a concern for personal autonomy. The cynical concept of consumer dependence or addiction would be detested by such an organization. Many of the Platonic criticisms of business that we have considered can be defused, if business would take seriously the values espoused by Peters and Waterman, and would use such enlightened managerial statesmen as Watson as models.

Generally, this type of management fits the requirements of such thinkers as Whitehead and Lodge, who consider a philosophical or holistic perspective in business to be essential for managerial wisdom, and it would clearly accord with the conception of justice entailed by the managerial creed. Not only will shareholders benefit from such an "excellent" company, but also the workers will "get their due" and the consumers will get quality and reliable products and services. Such business management will not be myopically dominated by the bottom line.

2. The Craftsmanship Model and Ethical Weaving

Our discussion has attempted to show how Platonic wisdom and justice follow from the values emphasized by Peters and Waterman, i.e., a craftsmanship model. But what of the other two cardinal virtues, courage and temperance? Can the craftsmanship value model serve as a source for ethical weaving? Can it properly balance courageous and temperate character traits yielding ethical managers and morally "excellent" corporations?

In speaking of a managerial theory for the 80's, Peters and Waterman emphasize a mixing of the goals of the courageous and temperate types. Stability is necessary with respect to basic values—an emphasis on excellent products and service (love of product, quality, production through people) and a value system that supports and implements them. Entrepreneurial attitudes and "habit breaking" are necessary because of business's need for the avoidance of stagnation ("calcification") through regular innovation. The concern for stability and security is mixed with entrepreneurial and "habit breaking" attitudes, according to these management theorists, by "excellent" companies emphasizing so-called "loose-tight properties." These companies are most rigid (tight) about their basic values (evidently, quality and reliable products and service and concern for people), and they demand and get conformity with regard to these values. The cultures of excellent companies, in this way, cater to organization man values; they cater to our security and stability needs and provide a sense of belongingness or meaning (purpose) to our lives. The excessive conformity and willingness to give up authority, which traditionally are concomitant with the above attitudes, are compensated for in excellent companies by an emphasis on creating environments in which employees can develop their abilities and on what Peters and Waterman call "autonomy"—the basis of the "loose" properties. The shared values provide a sense of purpose and stability, while the firms also encourage autonomy by allowing more experimentation and some failures.

It would seem that these "loose" properties are, themselves, entailed by the common values. A people orientation and, what I have called, a craftsmanship orientation help to create, as these authors maintain, an environment in which the development of people's abilities and "autonomy" are emphasized; basically, it seems that, according to Peters and Waterman, the "loose" properties—autonomy, innovation, entrepreneurship—are related to the craftsmanship orientation, i.e., an emphasis on quality. Such an emphasis leads, they maintain, to innovation; the drive to produce the best product and to do the best for the consumer creates a "focus" on innovation. Experimentation, as a part of their concept of autonomy, is also, they argue, a result of this emphasis on quality. Quality also leads to effectiveness—getting things done. It is the basis of a "turned-on, motivated, highly productive worker."[11] Generally, excitement, effectiveness, and autonomy, they maintain, go along with quality. It does seem that the development of these "loose" properties, associated with the courageous temperament, is aided by the application of a craftsmanship value system. In what follows, I shall elaborate upon Peters and Waterman's thesis concerning the mixing of courageous and temperate goals exhibited in "excellent" firms by showing how the craftsmanship model can be a basis for weaving together, in business leaders, courageous and temperate qualities manifested by businesspeople.

The craftsmanship model can be used to "weave" adequately the traits of temperate and courageous character types by correcting the tendency of each type to go to extremes and in so doing to temper each type with properties of the other type—to weave courageous and temperate properties together. According to Plato, as we have seen in Chapter 4, without such a tempering process there would be no moral leadership and, in our context, the formal business organization would suffer and eventually self-destruct.

We have seen that for Peters and Waterman, the emphasis on, and implementation of, shared values provide businesspeople with a sense of place, security, and stability; and a sense of belongingness (meaning and purpose in their lives) is derived from the specified higher, more "beautiful" values. Since traditionally, in the history of American business values, such values are associated with organization men, it is important to show that the craftsmanship model entailed by these shared values can control the development of extreme organization man traits and their consequent inadequate moral and organizational effects.

We saw that organization men exhibit traits of the excessively temperate type; they are submissive conformists who depend upon authority and who sacrifice courage and integrity for security (stability) and comfort. Craftsmen, however, are models of self-reliant individualists whose self-worth is based upon self-development. No wonder Peters and Waterman talk about autonomy as compensating for a willingness to conform and give up authority. Craftsmen are noted for their integrity, and instead of being motivated by fear (the stick), which nurtures cowardice, their conduct is guided by a concern for quality. Moreover, an excessive concern for security, comfort, and material goods are not basic values for the craftsman. Their complaint is often that the world is too materialistic, too concerned with comfort and security.

The superficiality of the organization man's values has been noted. In addition, organization men were seen to be bureaucrats who stick to the rules. Plato, we remember, maintains that temperate types are overly cautious and stick to precedents. In their extreme form, organization men reduce morality to a superficial concern for manners. This is, in part, due to a softness in character, an excessive concern for peace and order. An emphasis on excellence or quality, however, breeds the opposite of superficiality. Since a craftsmanship value system is based upon creating that which is substantive, rather than the appearance or image of that which is substantive, substantial rather than superficial human relations are emphasized. Finally, since craftsmen are not bureaucrats, their sense of "autonomy" will moderate the negative effects of bureaucratic tendencies in an organization.

Modern managers, especially in the upper echelons of big business, are not necessarily organization men. There is still admiration for the traditional individualistic American business character models, especially that of the robber baron. Moreover, we saw that, according to Maccoby, many modern upper echelon managers are gamesmen. Can the managerial craftsmanship ideal perform the same function with these models that it does with the organization man model? I think it can. I shall first show that the craftsmanship model can moderate the excessively courageous traits associated with the traditional American individualistic and materialistic ethic.

Plato, we remember, maintains that the tendency to brutality or bestiality (inhumanity) of the excessively courageous type must be tempered so that they become more just and concerned citizens. The warlike, e.g., extremely competitive tendencies especially must be moderated.

The selfishness associated with the frontier and robber baron forms of individualism will tend to be moderated by craftsmanship-type self-interest. (This will be developed in the section entitled, "The Craftsmanship Model and Self-Interest.") The excessive desire to win at all costs, using extremely competitive means, has tended to mold a hard, cold, unprincipled, and manipulative business character. Plato notes that courageous types, as opposed to temperate types, are not considered to be particularly fair. Even the gamesman, whom Maccoby thinks is a moral improvement on the traditional robber baron, exhibits, to some extent, the above negative moral traits. Winning, on this view, seems to take place within a zero-sum game. But for craftsmen, their competitiveness and desire to succeed benefit society as well as themselves. Indeed, craftsmen can be very competitive, but they do not compete by knocking others down. Craftsmen's competitiveness is directed toward achieving some standard of excellence. A craftsmanship ethic is essentially principled and nonmanipulative; creating something of value, not winning at all costs, is what counts.

Some of the excessively selfish, antisocial effects of the frontier and robber baron ethics can be modified by viewing individualism and being a part of some whole as compatible rather than as essentially in conflict. Modern business should define individuality, for its purposes, in terms of the development of the "parts" being provided for by the whole. The "whole" should be organized in such a way that business provides its employees with the opportunity to develop and express their capabilities. This, indeed, is the view of the Stanford School. This position builds upon the American concern for individuality but recognizes the need to modify traditional concepts in terms of modern business needs which, of course, are organizational. The rigidity of insisting upon following outmoded, rather than updated, definitions of traditional American business value concepts may be the most dangerous form of business inflexibility.

Lodge has written about the dangers of following anachronistic ideology. Ethical difficulties, he suggests, can arise from a conflict between anachronistic ideology and present practice. Managerial wisdom entails understanding the present ideology, helping to create an accord between practice and present ideology, and preserving what is best in the old ideology. For example, he suggests that the adversarial relationship between government and business, grounded in such anachronistic ideology as the limited state and property rights, has undermined a more realistic understanding of the support that government has given business. He also gives an example of the ethical dangers of what he calls "the go-it-alone propensity of business"—evidently influenced by the frontier and robber baron ethics. A well-intentioned friend of his, who owned a small paper company, infused with the spirit of private enterprise, spent $2.5 million in attempting to clean up the

Charles River in Boston. He was a failure because his anachronistic ideology blinded him to a more adequate solution.[12] Lodge's story puts us in mind of a more famous story told by Plato about Socrates. According to Plato, in the *Apology*, the priestess of the temple of Apollo at Delphi said that no one was wiser than Socrates. After questioning people who professed wisdom and showing them that they only thought that they possessed knowledge, Socrates recognized that his wisdom consisted in being conscious of his own ignorance.[13] Learning begins in recognizing one's own ignorance. Like Lodge's friend, Socrates' interlocutors do not question the values which are the presuppositions of their conduct, and it is the resulting lack of recognition of their own ignorance that logically prevents them from reaching correct conclusions.

Finally, one might use Maccoby's *The Leader* to reinforce the benefits of the craftsmanship model. Of the six models of leadership he considers in this book, three are gamesmen.[14] In each case, however, they differ from traditional gamesmen in that adherence to the craftsmanship model has tempered the negative moral and organizational effects of the excessively courageous, traditional gamesman and, in consequence, has yielded both a more moral and a more successful leader.[15]

3. The Craftsmanship Model, Materialism, and Morality

We have seen how a Peters and Waterman/ Watson model can help to create a firm that conforms to the Platonic standard for a virtuous organization. However, it is also helpful to show that the moral superiority of the craftsmanship model over the traditional models that characterize American business is, in part, related to the basically nonmaterialistic motivation of the craftsman. The advantages of being immoral, e.g., stealing, cheating, lying are obvious to a person whose values are predominantly materialistic. As suggested in Chapter 1, if we can get away with such immoral conduct, we will profit in a narrow materialistic sense. However, it is clear that immorality, and the intemperance that often accompanies it, is not advantageous to a lover of craftsmanship. Immorality and the indulgence of the appetites diminish rather than enhance craftsmanship and, therefore, detract from the craftsman's source of happiness. That is, intemperance and immorality in general, insofar as such conduct is directed toward materialistic goals, distract us from the goal of quality and diminish the sense of pride and satisfaction we derive from it. Maccoby's experience with craftsmen confirms the fact that they are scrupulously honest, and that they essentially respect other people.

The craftsmanship model can also be shown to be morally superior to traditional American business character models by contrasting the types of self-interest underlying American business conduct with the type of self-interest entailed by the craftsmanship model. The former types of self-interest leave a great deal to be desired from a moral standpoint while the latter type of self-interest has positive moral implications. In the next section, I shall examine the relation between American business and self-interest, and in the one which follows that section, the connection between self-interest and the craftsmanship model. In both sections, the ethical implications of the respective types of self-interest are emphasized.

4. American Business and Self-Interest

In *Religion and the Rise of Capitalism*, Tawney argues that the Puritan ethic converts a "natural frailty" ("the insistence among men of pecuniary motives, the strength of economic egotism, the appetite for gain") "into a resounding virtue."[16] More generally, he maintains that the American business tradition refuses to call vices and virtues by their "right names."[17] The supposed harmony between materialistic self-interest (and business success) and virtue (the Protestant ethic) and, more generally, the attempt to make narrow self-interest into a positive social and ethical as well as economic force in laissez-faire theory and Social Darwinism are glaring examples of wishful thinking by the American business tradition. Possibly, a sounder conception of business requires the rejection of the pessimism concerning human nature which underlies traditional American business and the restoration of a conception of virtue that is worthy of its name.

But before I develop this point, it might be helpful to consider the importance of narrow self-interest to American business. The classical view of corporate social responsibility, mentioned briefly in Chapter 5, is based upon laissez-faire theory. Actually, the implied narrow self-interest view of human nature was not endorsed by Adam Smith.[18] Nonetheless, the classical theory draws its economic and social justification from laissez-faire theory. According to the classical theory, although the businessperson is motivated by the pursuit of profit, he has little power over marketplace transactions. A free, competitive business context guides business activities, by an "invisible hand," to an economically just and socially propitious result. This theory also maintains that the shareholders, as owners of private property, have the right, within the bounds of the law, to do as they please with their property, i.e., seek to maximize profit. Thus, according to this view, business has no social responsibilities other than to produce goods and services efficiently, make money for shareholders, and conduct business in a lawful manner. Friedman, the most famous exponent of this view, therefore argues that the only social responsibility business has is to maximize profits.[19]

In *Ethics and Profits*, Silk and Vogel, on the basis of seminars conducted with 360 business leaders, argue that this view is the dominant one among upper echelon executives.[20] Although there are surveys that conflict with this view, it is accepted, often with regret, by a number of commentators on the business scene. Nonetheless, as Lodge, Silk, Vogel, and others have argued, this position is anachronistic. It is based upon the following beliefs: a competitive market, the corporation as the private property of its owners (shareholders), limited participation of government in the economy, and the separation of the economic and social spheres of society. Given the popularity of the classical view among business leaders, it is no wonder that Irving Kristol, Lodge, Silk, Vogel, and others have questioned the ideology of many of our business leaders.

To elaborate briefly on the above difficulties, laissez-faire theory was designed to apply to small businesses in an openly competitive context. As I suggested in Chapter 5, Smith's theory was not designed to apply to a business world dominated by large corporations. Moreover, large businesses do not compete in the way small businesses do; that is, price, product, and quality competition is perceived by managers of large corporations as being ruinous to big business. Nor can it be argued that since managers are employees of the owners of corporations (shareholders) their sole objective should be to serve the interests of shareholders. Even if we put aside the debatable view that the right of private property applies in the corporate context in the same way in which it applies in an individual context, it is confusing to think of a large corporation as the private property of shareholders.

Unlike small businesses, they are sanctioned by the government, and it would contradict the purpose of government to sanction corporations whose operations have substantial negative social impact. It is also confusing, as I have argued, to conceive of such corporations as purely economic, rather than quasi-social and political, institutions. They are not self-regulating for the common good and they affect too many people. Finally, it is naive to conceive of modern American society in terms of limited participation of government in the economy.

I should think that modern business leaders often appeal to an enlightened, rather than a narrow, self-interest. Elton Mayo was instrumental in impressing upon business leaders the importance of this type of self-interest. Eventually, under the influence of his experiments and theories, employees were given all sorts of benefits, because paternalism was thought to serve the narrow goals (profit and productivity) of the large corporation. One important effect of this was the creation of the organization man. However, as we have seen, this business character model is a failure from a moral point of view and, therefore, cannot serve as a model for socially responsible management.

To elaborate somewhat on the importance of enlightened self-interest to corporate leaders, it may be noted that such famous businesspeople as Reginald Jones (G.E.), Richard Gustenberg, and Edward Cole (G.M.)—to mention a few—disagree with the narrow materialistic self-interest orientation of the classical view. Although they do believe that self-interest dominates the attitude of business management, they think that it should be a broader or more enlightened self-interest which is based upon paying close attention to public consensus. This view of corporate social responsibility seems to be based upon the belief that managers who adopt this position will avoid or, at least, reduce government regulation and public criticism and, more positively, create public good will by enhancing the public image of the corporation (this is perceived as essential to the survival and well-being of the corporation). Two important points ought to be mentioned in evaluating this position.

Depending upon the largesse of corporations is dangerous. Changing circumstances may convince management that benefits meted out to various spheres of interest, whether it be employees or the public at large, are no longer advantageous to the corporation or cannot be easily supported and therefore should be dropped.

The above form of corporate social responsibility entails a superficial, rather than a deeply committed, morality. It would be foolish not to be on our guard, indeed, not to be skeptical of the constancy and stability of managerial altruism. This leads us to a second, and possibly more crucial, criticism. If, on the above view, the ethical relationship between management and the spheres of interest affected by management tends to be superficial, there is a strong tendency for management to substitute image for substance. Indeed, public image and the public relations used to enhance it are essential to this view of corporate social responsibility. On this view, then, one should suspect that image and rhetoric are often substituted for substantial benefits. Unfortunately, business activities provide all too many illustrations of this point. Thus, Douglas A. Hayes argues that although there are exceptions, corporate concern for public welfare does not extend beyond projecting a favorable image for the purpose of public relations. He correctly warns corporate leaders that mere rhetoric creates a credibility gap—a gap to which the public, today, is particularly sensitive.[21]

5. The Craftsmanship Model and Self-Interest

If neither narrow self-interest nor enlightened self-interest, and their related theories of corporate social responsibility, is adequate from an ethical point of view, must we, then, abandon an appeal to self-interest if we are to develop an ethical organization? I do not think so.

Drucker, the father of modern business management theory, defines the purpose of business in terms of supplying the wants and needs of customers, rather than profit maximization; therefore, its goal should be better and more economic goods and services.[22] Indeed, if businesspeople wish to be treated as professionals, this should be the definition of business. By the definition of a professional, his or her knowledge or skill should be directed to the benefit of other people. This is why professionals want to and deserve to get paid; they give service. (This point will be considered again in Appendix I.)

Our ideal of a managerial craftsman fits the above model of a professional. But it does not fit Tawney's notion of the traditional American business leader. Craftsmen of any sort do not turn a vice, narrow or materialistic self-interest, into a virtue. The reason for this is that the self-interest of a craftsman differs from such narrow self-interest. Craftsmanship self-interest also differs from enlightened self-interest as discussed above. The craftsmanship model entails self-interested motivations, but such self-interest, which is equated with a concern for self-development, should not be viewed as opposed to other people's interests.

The concept of socially responsible management implies that management is willing to take responsibility for its actions. Lawrence M. Miller contrasts managers who have an excellence orientation with those who do not. The former, he argues, are prone to take responsibility for their conduct while the latter often blame forces outside of their control for activity that goes astray, e.g., unions, corporate staff, the economy. He calls this tendency of management to externalize responsibility "a cultural disease in corporations." However, he maintains that the attitude of the manager who has a sense of excellence is quite the opposite.

> This displacement of responsibility is a force in direct contradiction to the achievement of excellence. Managers who achieve excellence respond to events in a highly internal manner. They see themselves in control of things, responsible for the way they are, good or bad.[23]

Obviously, a concern for excellence benefits society, not to mention management itself, by providing, in the case of business, quality goods and services. But the connection between this sort of self-interest and other people's interest is psychologically and ethically deeper than one might suspect. On the craftsmanship model of self-interest, there is no clear demarcation between acting on self-interest and acting from a concern for others; that is, here, the opposition between self-interest and altruistic motives is nonexistent. This type of self-interest relates to a concern for human dignity and worth. The concern for our own worth and dignity extends, especially with proper nurturing, to a concern for human dignity generally. An ethic can, then, be developed which prohibits human manipulation, and more positively, helps to nurture respect and concern for people's potentialities. Maccoby's experience with craftsman types confirms this. It is important to understand that giving, on this view of self-interest, is of a different nature from the type of giving that is based upon enlightened self-interest. Since craftsmanship, as I use the term, is a way of expressing what one thinks are the better parts of oneself, what gives one pride and dignity, giving to others has a natural quality (which is absent from enlightened self-interest). Giving is an expression of oneself, one's accomplishments, in the world. Thus, for example, the dedicated teacher gives of himself or herself from a love of learning. Generally, the craftsman wants to present his work as an expression of the best of himself or herself. Again, we see the moral superiority of a craftsmanship model of business management over those that have been exhibited in the history of American business values.

If I am correct about the moral and social implications of a craftsmanship value system, this individualistic ethic would tend to moderate the values of the more antihumanistic traditional American business ethic. Material success and lack of success does not symbolize virtue and vice respectively, any more than so-called pride in ownership, conspicuous consumption, societal honors (reputation, esteem, prestige, power, and the like) symbolize the worth of a human being. Craftsmanship values correctly emphasize the fact that human worth is based upon intrinsic rather than extrinsic values.

6. Craftsmanship Self-Interest and Modern Psychology

The view of self-interest that pertains to the craftsmanship model accords well with the position of modern industrial psychologists. Abraham H. Maslow, for example, postulates different levels of needs—the satisfaction of higher levels requiring the previous satisfaction of lower levels. The fifth, or highest level, is said to be the need for self-actualization, which accords with our model. However, in the 1960's and 70's, it was Douglas McGregor who had the most influence on management. He argues that traditional managers accept certain pessimistic assumptions about human nature which they apply to employees—he calls this theory X. According to this theory, employees avoid responsibility (they prefer to be ordered by superiors), do not like work and are unambitious, and are basically motivated by security needs rather than concern for their firms. But, he argues, theory X is an incorrect view of human nature and, therefore, yields minimal results. He contrasts theory X with theory Y—a position that, according to McGregor, entails a more optimistic and correct view of human nature. It maintains that work can be a basic source of satisfaction, and workers are capable of self-direction or autonomy.[24]

This view, clearly, accords with our craftsmanship model. He argues that management has incorrectly emphasized extrinsic, rather than intrinsic, rewards. McGregor argues that once physical needs are satisfied, higher order needs will be perceived as goals. In the context of corporate life, meaningful careers become of paramount importance. He recognizes the dangers, both to the individual and the firm, of corporate manipulation; a deep mistrust of the system is engendered by merely paying lip service to higher human needs. His critique of corporate paternalism accords with the position for which I have argued. "A paternalistic strategy," he argues, "in fact involves control of extrinsic rewards.... It is not the creation of an environment that provides opportunities for intrinsic rewards. Therefore, a paternalistic strategy does not in my view create conditions for self-actualization."[25] A number of industrial psychologists, the most influential of whom is Frederick Herzberg, agree with the thrust of McGregor's argument.[26]

7. The Generic Concept of Craftsmanship and Business Leadership

It might be objected that the craftsman is not a good model for corporate management. We shall see, in the Postscript, that Veblen was an admirer of craftsmanship. Mills, in an introduction to Veblen's *Theory of the Working Class*, says, "for in truth, Veblen's 'workmanship' is an ideal set forth by a man afraid to set forth ideals, and it is more socially at home in some simple artisans society than in the modern social disorder we are trying to live in and understand."[27] There is a sense in which this is true. Plato's early city in the *Republic*, the city of pigs, is just such an ideal. Yet Plato is able to extrapolate basic features of craftsmanship and use such features as the foundation for his model of God—the *Demiourgos* of the *Timaeus*. Of course, God is not Veblen's engineer or some carpenter. Nonetheless, as I have argued, such Platonic analogical reasoning is most helpful in formulating an adequate model of statesmanlike management. In doing this, one must abstract from certain traits of specific types of craftsmen. When this is done one can derive what I have called a generic concept of craftsmanship based upon its goal (quality or excellence) and motivations (personal satisfaction, pride in accomplishment, and dignity that is grounded in a concern for self-development). We have seen that the craftsman's nonmaterialistic values and the connection between a craftsmanship type of self-interest and altruism have important implications for justice and morality in general. Moreover, autonomy, innovation, and entrepreneurship, according to Peters and Waterman, are related to an emphasis on quality. These points are based upon the generic concept of craftsmanship. Self-reliance derived from self-development (autonomy), integrity, emphasis on substance rather than appearance, as well as a nonmaterialistic orientation—all related to craftsmanship in the generic sense—moderate extreme organization man values. Again, emphasis on nonmaterialistic values, craftsmanship self-interest, craftsmanlike competitiveness—related to craftsmanship in the generic sense —moderates the extremes of the traditional American business ethic.

In *White Collar*, Mills argues that, in the modern world, craftsmanship is an anachronism. "As ethic," he says, "craftsmanship is confined to minuscule groups of privileged professionals and intellectuals."[28] This is interesting for, as have I suggested, the notion of a managerial craftsman fits the model of the professional. Second, intellectuality entails a liberal arts orientation, and this implies a love of leisure and play. Mills argues that, for craftsmen, there is no split between work and play.[29] Insofar as the liberal arts is necessary for business statesmanship, and I have argued that this is so, a craftsmanship orientation aids, rather than hinders, such an ideal. Moreover, it is an aid to business statesmanship in another way. We have seen that managerial statesmanship (wisdom) entails knowledge of an organized whole and what is good for that whole. Of course, the generic idea of craftsmanship is not a sufficient condition for managerial statesmanship. This generic idea must be supplemented by the knowledge necessary for proper managerial leadership. But not only is this generic idea necessary, according to Peters and Waterman, for producing proper managerial values, it entails a predisposition for dealing with the whole rather than merely the parts. Mills, correctly I think, says that "the craftsman has an image of the completed product, and even though he does not make it all [assuming that he does not], he sees the place of his part in the whole, and thus understands the meaning of his exertion in terms of the whole."[30] Thus, craftsmanship, in an interesting way, is tied to the holistic attitude necessary for managerial statesmanship.

Given my use of the term "craftsmanship," then, it is important to distinguish between generic and specific types of craftsmanship. Thus, for example, Maccoby may be correct in distinguishing between dutiful and receptive craftsmen. "The difference is that the dutiful are more driven, compulsive, and hierarchical, while the receptive are more life-loving, tolerant, and democratic."[31] However, such a concrete analysis of specific craftsmen would be unhelpful and misleading in my context. More to the point is his discussion of basic craftsmanlike attitudes that underlie the values of some managers. A clear example of what I am *not* talking about is David L. Bradford and Allan R. Cohen's analysis of the manager as master technician. The model is "the master craftsman who knew all aspects of the trade and passed it on to apprentices."[32] For example, in some entrepreneurial high-tech firms, the models are chief designer managers. They are looked upon as having all the answers and subordinates feed information to them. Such managers, they argue, can undermine subordinates' confidence and possibilities for growth by always doing things better than them or by supervising them too closely. Moreover, they argue that "technicians do not respond well to human problems which require flexibility, improvisation, listening and patience."[33] Their basic source of satisfaction is in their specialized field and not in managing people. Possibly the craftsman qua modern engineer or technician may best accord with this model. If this is the case, Bradford and Cohen's analysis is appropriate. But it is irrelevant to what I am doing, for they analyze the traits of a specific type of craftsman rather than providing a generic model for craftsmanship.

A counterexample to Bradford and Cohen's, provided by Lawrence Miller, illustrates how adherence to the generic concept of craftsmanship can help one to change the negative traits encountered in Bradford and Cohen's manager as master technician. Since we have seen that self-development is the subjective counterpart of excellence as the goal of craftsmanship in the generic sense, Miller is correct when he argues that "excellence results from an ability to learn, an ability to respond to one's environment in productive ways."[34] This model entails, as a motivation, satisfaction from the "process of self-improvement" rather than from the "symbols of success."[35] Let us, then, consider how this implication of the generic idea of craftsmanship applies to Miller's example of a so-called manager as master technician.

Miller presents such an example in the person of a Jim Wilson. He is a scientist with a Ph.D. and many years of experience in high technology. Although well-liked and respected by subordinates, they did offer some criticism of him which paralleled the objections to the negative attributes of Bradford and Cohen's chief designer manager. Wilson, according to his subordinates, could be "very authoritarian" and "impatient with others who were not as quick as he was."[36] However, instead of taking the position that Bradford and Cohen do, Miller shows how Wilson's concern for self-improvement (related to the generic concept of craftsmanship) helped him to respond positively to the above criticisms. On hearing these negative comments about himself,

> he [Wilson] wanted to know exactly what was meant by 'authoritarian'. He wanted to know in what situations, with which level of people, and how could he have handled the situation differently? He was processing every bit of feedback with the intelligence that had apparently characterized his entire career. I learned later from people close to him that he was making deliberate efforts to improve in these areas and even acknowledging his faults in open sessions. His efforts to address his own deficiencies served as a model again for others in the organization.[37]

NOTES

1. Richard T. Pascale, "The Paradox of 'Corporate Culture': Reconciling Ourselves to Socialization," *California Management Review* (Winter 1985): p. 29.

2. Richard T. Pascale and Anthony G. Athos, *The Art of Japanese Management: Applications for American Executives* (New York: Warner Books, 1981).

3. William G. Ouchi, *Theory Z: How Business Can Meet The Japanese Challenge* (Reading, Mass.: Addison-Wesley, 1981).

4. Peters and Waterman argue that excellent companies are initially based upon excellent leadership, and this leadership provides for the development of cultures which inculcate the leader's values as shared values. These values are transmitted by means of stories, myths, and legends about the leaders. Thomas J. Peters and Robert H. Waterman Jr., *In Search of Excellence: Lessons from America's Best-Run Companies* (New York: Harper and Row, 1982), p. 75. See, also, Terrence E. Deal and Allan A. Kennedy's position discussed in Appendix II.

5. Pascale and Athos, p. 50.

6. Peters and Waterman, p. 37.

7. Peters, Waterman, Pascale and Athos stress Thomas Watson's belief that the value system of a company and how faithfully the organization implements it have more to do with its success or failure than does technology, organizational structure or even economic performance. Ouchi also emphasizes this position.

8. It is rather clear that Plato would be sympathetic to the idea of a craftsmanlike statesman. For Plato, the model for statesmanship of the highest kind would be found in his cosmological treatise, the *Timaeus*. Here, the creator of the universe is said to be a *demiourgos*—a craftsman (*Timaeus* 28–29). In the *Statesman*, Plato compares the statesman to a master-builder (259e–260a), and as a craftsman, he or she is like a weaver (305ff). However, since a statesman, for Plato, is also a philosopher, the statesman-craftsman must also be philosophical—in the language of the *Republic*, a philosopher-king. The *Demiourgos* creates the world from the best possible pattern or model (*Timaeus* 28–29); the world is a sensible copy of the ideal. Similarly, Plato's philosopher-king appeals to the best possible model—the pattern of Plato's ideal city—in crafting a society that is virtuous and happy; he is the true "craftsman of temperance, justice, and every civil virtue" (*Republic* 500c–d).

9. R. G. Collingwood, who provides a helpful analysis of craftsmanship in *The Principles of Art* (New York: Oxford University Press, 1958), argues that craftsmen produce things because there is a demand for them, and they aim to satisfy customer's demands (p. 18). The ideal of craftsmanship, then, entails the satisfaction of demands by quality products. It is interesting to note that this analysis accords well with Drucker's view of the goal of business which will be considered later in this chapter.

10. The notion of management as a craft would have been accepted by Aristotle as well as Plato. Indeed, Aristotle begins the *Nicomachean Ethics* with the ideal of a hierarchy of crafts, with the highest craft, statecraft, at its apex. Each craft, in the hierarchy, produces something of value, some good. Since the master craft, statesmanship, entails knowledge of the highest good, subordinate crafts, which serve the interests of the whole by playing their part, are guided by this wisdom

for the good of the whole (*Nicomachean Ethics* 1094a1–b10). I take this to be a fair description of managerial statesmanship.

11. Peters and Waterman, p. 321.

12. George C. Lodge, "The Connection between Ethics and Ideology," *Journal of Business Ethics* (1982): 85–98.

13. *Apology* 21a–22e.

14. Michael Maccoby, *The Leader: A New Face for American Management* (New York: Simon and Schuster, 1981).

15. Maccoby says the following about these three gamesmen. Stan Lunine, a congressman and mayor, is a gamesman who is concerned with people; he attempts to undermine a sense of hopelessness by helping people to fulfill themselves. Pehr Gyllenhammer, a CEO, is a typical gamesman in that he can innovate, experiment, and relate to a changing market, but unlike the typical gamesman, he is concerned with human self-development. Paul Reaves, a foreman, has traits of the typical gamesman—love of adventure, innovation, and risktaking. But unlike the typical gamesman, he is concerned with developing people's potentialities. Generally, Maccoby argues, the philosophy of management of his model leaders is rooted in a concern for human development and the consequent outrage concerning wasted human potential.

16. R. H. Tawney, *Religion and The Rise of Capitalism: A Historical Study* (New York: Mentor Book, 1926), p. 205.

17. Tawney says that at least the medieval church "had not learned to persuade themselves that greed was enterprise and avarice economy" (Tawney, p. 58).

18. The view of human nature suggested by the classical view is certainly not the position that Adam Smith intended. The conduct of businesspeople, acting out of self-interest in a free or competitive market, according to Smith, will lead through the guidance of the mechanism of supply and demand to a common good. But, first, he was suspicious of the narrow self-interest of businesspeople. Second, Smith was no Hobbesian about human nature. He believed that there is a certain wisdom in nature; that is, nature can be trusted, for it exhibits a certain balance. No wonder Smith was ready to appeal to a natural principle, rather than government, for guidance in business affairs. His view of human nature is found in his *Theory of Moral Sentiments*. Smith maintains that people are motivated by sympathy as well

as narrow self-interest. Sympathy, which allows one to imagine himself in another's place and vicariously participate in his feelings, is a basis for moral conduct, for it moderates the force of narrow self-interest. Virtue, for Smith, was not simply the negative Hobbesian form of virtue—don't hurt your fellow human beings for, if you do, you will be punished. Hobbesian morality, according to Smith, rests on the paradox of defining a virtue, justice, in terms of resentment; in this sense, it is based upon "latent animosity." Smith, then, analyzes human nature in a more balanced way than does Hobbes. Human beings are by nature both egotistic and altruistic, moved by both a love of self and by fellow-feeling for others.

19. Milton Friedman, "The Social Responsibility of Business Is To Increase Its Profits," *New York Times Magazine* (September 13 1970).

20. Leonard S. Silk and David Vogel, *Ethics and Profits* (New York: Simon and Schuster, 1976).

21. Douglas A. Hayes, "A Case For Social Responsibility," In *Issues in Business and Society*, eds. George A. Steiner and John A. Steiner, 2nd ed. (New York: Random House, 1977), pp. 175–180.

22. Drucker's views on the purpose of business and the function of profit in business can be found, for example, in Peter F. Drucker, *People and Performance: the Best of Peter Drucker on Management* (New York: Harper and Row, 1977), pp. 90, 97–99, 122–125.

23. Lawrence M. Miller, *American Spirit: Visions of a New Corporate Culture* (New York: Warner Books, 1984), pp. 64–65.

24. See "The Human Side of Enterprise" in *Leadership and Motivation: Essays of Douglas McGregor*, eds. Warren G. Bennis and Edgar H. Schein (Cambridge, Mass.: The M. I. T. Press, 1966).

25. Douglas McGregor, *The Professional Manager*, eds. Caroline McGregor and Warren G. Bennis (New York: McGraw Hill, 1967, published posthumously), p. 77.

26. In spite of the emphasis on a more optimistic view of human nature, which I think has considerable merit, many thinkers still believe that this "academic" position is too unrealistic. Stanton, for example, argues as follows: For many employees, work is not the most important part of their lives; it is a means to an end, e.g., leisure and/or family activities. There is more relativity in values than

McGregor *et al* are willing to admit. Job autonomy is important to some employees, but others require highly structured unambiguous work. Moreover, money is not emphasized enough by these more idealistic thinkers. The strong humanistic values underlying these more optimistic theories tend to overidealize worker's abilities or talents and, therefore, their potential contribution to a firm. See Erwin S. Stanton, *Reality-Centered People Management: Key to Improved Productivity* (New York: Amacon, 1982).

27. See C. Wright Mills's introduction to Thorstein Veblen, *The Theory of the Leisure Class* (New York: Mentor Book, 1953), p. XVIII.

28. C. Wright Mills, *White Collar: The American Middle Classes* (New York: Oxford University Press, 1956), p. 224.

29. Mills, p. 222.

30. Mills, p. 221.

31. Michael Maccoby, *The Gamesman: The New Corporate Leaders* (New York: Simon and Schuster, 1976), p. 54.

32. David L. Bradford and Allan R. Cohen, *Managing for Excellence: The Guide to Developing High Performance in Contemporary Organizations* (New York, John Wiley and Sons, 1984), p. 33.

33. Bradford and Cohen, p. 41.

34. Lawrence Miller, p. 54.

35. Lawrence Miller, p. 54.

36. Lawrence Miller, p. 53.

37. Lawrence Miller, p. 54.

CHAPTER VII

POSTSCRIPT

1. The Practicality of the Craftsmanship Model

One possible objection to my argument in Chapter 6 is that it may be all well and good, but it is typical pie-in-the-sky philosophy. How can such a model be implemented in modern business? Many business commentators have argued that few careers, even at the managerial level, really tap human potentials, and most get so repetitive (and, therefore, boring) that after a while little satisfaction and pride can be derived from work. No wonder that craftsman types in corporations criticize their work as not yielding enough satisfaction. Moreover, I have mentioned the belief that management's basic problems relate to people, and the more machine-like people are, the easier the corporation is to manage. Individuality and creativity, associated with craftsmanship, tend to suffer as a consequence. It is also maintained that large organizations, under conditions of oligopoly, not only have no incentive to price or product competition, they do not want to engage in quality competition, for that too can be potentially ruinous. Finally, concern for organizational efficiency and growth does not encourage the corporate executive to be interested in the product for its own sake, and emphasis on cost reductions provides a real incentive to lowering quality.

Drucker, in *Technology, Management and Society*, lists what he calls a new set of assumptions to fit today's realities and speaks of how business, and other organizations, will have to adapt organizations to the needs, aspirations, and potentials of the individual rather than adapting the individual to the demands of the organizations, if only for the purpose of surviving.[1] The craftsmanship model clearly emphasizes individual development. Second, the "knowledge worker" is fast becoming business's basic capital resource, and self-development and its correlate quality have always been hallmarks of people whose career is based on developing knowledge. Drucker argues that the "knowledge worker" (the largest group in the American labor force) is motivated primarily by a sense of achievement. Therefore, a craftsmanship model should be implemented, if business wants to prevent the alienation of this type of worker.

In the 1980's, there has been much criticism of the view that organizations must strive for increased specialization because this increases efficiency and productivity. This passion for specialization is, clearly, one reason for the difficulty in implementing our model, e.g., human potentials are not tapped, work is boring (because it is repetitive), and little satisfaction or pride is derived from work. Ouchi, in *Theory Z*, argues that overspecialization in American firms—a product of bureaucratic forms of organization—breeds loyalty to the specialty rather than to the entire firm, and this leads to lack of knowledge of problems in other specialties which hinders the proper management of others. According to Ouchi, Japanese-style companies achieve higher productivity than the more bureaucratic American firms with lower specialization.[2]

The increased concern for quality products is derived, it would seem, primarily from the success of the Japanese emphasis on quality. Many firms are demanding that their managers be responsible for quality at all levels of the organization. Although traditional business wisdom views quality and productivity as conflicting, the truth, according to the Stanford School, is that increasing quality, increases productivity. My position is that some difficulties encountered by American business competing on the basis of quality are caused by the values of managers. Problems concerning quality can be traced to inadequate managerial leadership. Those who believe that the model I am suggesting is typical pie-in-the-sky philosophy ought, probably, to look again at its ultimate bottom line benefits.

2. The Craftsmanship Model and Culture

I have argued that it is easier to implement a character model if it is grounded somewhere in one's culture. Maccoby, in *The Leader*, argues that a craft ethic is a dominant American type (one of the four American ethics), and he attributes its articulation to Benjamin Franklin.[3] I do not think that this model is part of the dominant traditional American ethic. Therefore, the attempt to implement such an ethic will, at least to some extent, go against our cultural grain, and the difficulty of such an implementation should not be underestimated.

Maccoby seems to broaden the concept of a craft ethic to include self-employed farmers and businessmen, and by so doing tends to confuse different types.[4] On the other hand, his concept is narrower than mine, for he restricts it to a specific preindustrial American type.[5] Veblen presents a different picture. He argues that the American farmer is a pioneer and not a craftsman; the passion for acquisition drives him to work. Franklin equates commerce with cheating, and his list of virtues is not, contrary to what Maccoby suggests, a list of craft virtues; they are, rather, those basically attributed to the farmer as small entrepreneur or capitalist. Second, Franklin extols labor as activity which prevents vice from creeping into the soul through idleness and as a means to comfortable living; he does not praise labor for its intrinsic worth as a real craftsman would.[6]

The facts, then, as I understand them, lead to the conclusion that a proper craft ethic has not been particularly dominant in this country and certainly does not rival the Protestant ethic. The Protestant ethic was never a craft ethic, and as Veblen shows in *The Instinct of Workmanship and the State of the Industrial Arts*, commerce or business emphasizes monetary or fiscal matters and does not particularly value workmanship or even the technical side of business. Under the guild system, the craftsman was a combination of craftsman and trader (of his wares), and he valued himself as a serviceable member of society—he produced for human use—which I may note is a mark of a professional.

With the breakdown of the handicraft system, business (trade) was differentiated from workmanship and everything, including the efficiency of workmanship, was measured by monetary standards. Veblen calls this the contamination of the instinct of workmanship by the ideal of self-aggrandizement. Industrialization, of course, made things difficult for craftsmen. The owners who controlled craftsmen were not themselves craftsmen, and technology, which is basic to industrialization, is not modeled on craftsmanship—change is not guided by a deliberate process leading to a specified purpose nor is it infused with personality.[7] It might be helpful to let Veblen speak for himself:

> Habituation to bargaining and to the competitive principles of business necessarily brings it about that pecuniary standards of efficiency invade (contaminate) the sense of workmanship; so that, workmen, equipment and products come to be rated on a scale of money values, which has only a circuitous and often only a putative relation to their workmanlike efficiency or their serviceability.... Workmanship comes to be confused with salesmanship, until tact, effrontery and prevarication have come to serve as a standard of efficiency, and unearned gain is accepted as the measure of productiveness.[8]

The lack of competitive practices in modern corporate business is sometimes said to lead to the same result, a deemphasis on quality. The modern corporate executive, functioning under conditions of oligopoly, seems to have as little concern for quality as Veblen's capitalist. I have mentioned that, under such conditions, the giant corporations have no incentive to compete in quality, any more than in price or products. Such competition, as Graham Bannock suggests, is perceived as "potentially ruinous."[9] The large firm is interested in efficiency and growth rather than the quality of a product. It is sometimes felt that the best engineers are involved in planned obsolescence.

Peters, in *Thriving on Chaos*, discusses the perceived gap in quality between, for example, Japanese and American goods and services. "For the most part, the quality of made-in-America goods and services is questionable; perhaps 'stinks' is often a more accurate word. Yet, fifteen years after the battering began, quality is still not often truly at the top of the American corporate agenda."[10] He argues for what, by this time, is well known—customers will pay for quality, firms that provide quality goods and services thrive, and workers "become energized by the opportunity to provide a top-quality product or service."[11] Nonetheless, business-people resist the facts about quality. He says,

> I still encounter such skepticism among U.S. executives [about the importance of quality].... 'Where's your evidence?' they commonly ask.... I produce the evidence. And yet, as often as not, though I cite the source and produce the originals of the studies I still get blank stares; and not infrequently, in the face of the hard evidence, the skepticism is not only not removed,

but turns to raw belligerence of the 'it's just not so' variety. Then, I usually get very quiet—because I am scared.[12]

To what can one attribute such resistance in the face of obvious facts? The probable answer is that it is contrary to the values with which these executives were brought up. Peters suggests this when he indicates that habits of valuing quality are cultural. "The Japanese aesthetic sense is centuries old. Within the Toyota or Sony Walkman lie the modern outcroppings of the tea ceremony."[13] The Japanese are "finicky customers" when it comes to quality.

Peters's problem, in an interesting way, relates to the possibility of being entrepreneurial. It is very difficult, as I suggested, to counteract deep cultural biases. A basic criticism of strong corporate cultures is that they are not receptive to change. However, one of the advantages of strong corporate cultures is that, recognizing the force of culture, they can build into the culture of their firm emphasis on flexibility and innovation, constructive confrontation, creative conflict, and the like. (This issue will be discussed in Appendix II.) People can learn to cope constructively, rather than destructively, with change. This is an example of being entrepreneurial in Drucker's sense. That is, where some people see problems, others see opportunities. If left to its own devices, business will often "solve" problems created by its culture by appealing, often unconsciously, to other facets of its culture. We saw this in the modification of organization man qualities by those of the robber baron, creating the gamesman. But if we take a truly businesslike approach, we must manage change. If a change to a more craftsmanlike character model is necessary, and such a model is not dominant in American business culture, we must create a culture to counteract the forces which will undermine it. Since strong corporate culture advocates recognize the force of culture, they also recognize the difficulties involved and emphasize the danger of a quick-fix approach. The skepticism about the importance of quality, encountered by Peters, is, after all, a product of the upbringing of these CEOs. The destructive prejudices bred by anachronistic values and dogmatic frames of mind must be counteracted by creating a healthy counterculture which, as I have argued, emphasizes the liberal arts or humanistic values as well as craftsmanship values. Being entrepreneurial itself should be looked at in new ways. The traditional entrepreneurial model is that of the robber baron. Thus, an entrepreneur is often thought to combine the qualities of the inventor and risktaker. Drucker calls this the 19th century form of entrepreneurship. Successful contemporary entrepreneurs, he thinks, are opportunity focused, not risk focused. They minimize risk by managing change in such a way as to exploit it as an opportunity. Moreover, he thinks that "bright ideas" are usually not the basis of successful corporate innovations; nor are the newest, most advanced, most technically sophisticated high-tech products necessarily what the consumer deems of basic value. We saw that Plato defines courage in terms of knowledge—knowledge of what is and what is not dangerous. Successful entrepreneurs act on the basis of knowledge, not guts alone. Entrepreneurship, according to Drucker, entails lifelong learning as well as habits of flexibility, hard work, and self-discipline. The knowledge gained is necessary in order to go, so to speak, with the flow. Such learning makes the entrepreneur an astute diagnostician of the areas of change that offer opportunities.[14] Such an attitude, I would argue, is what is necessary in undermining the mentality that scares Peters so much.

NOTES

1. Peter F. Drucker, *Technology, Management and Society: Essays by Peter F. Drucker* (New York: Harper and Row, 1970), pp. 32–42.

2. William G. Ouchi, *Theory Z: How Business Can Meet The Japanese Challenge* (Reading, Mass.: Addison-Wesley, 1981), pp. 31–32, 220.

3. Michael Maccoby, *The Leader: A New Face for American Management* (New York: Simon and Schuster, 1981), p. 26.

4. Maccoby, pp. 26–27.

5. Maccoby, pp. 27, 29–30.

6. There is a sense in which Franklin's conception of virtue conflicts with craft virtue in my sense. Weber says, "According to Franklin, those virtues [honesty, punctuality, industry, frugality], like all others, are only in so far virtues as they are actually useful to the individual, and the surrogate of mere appearance is always sufficient when it accomplishes the end in view." Max Weber, *The Protestant Ethic and the Spirit of Capitalism*, trans. Talcott Parsons (New York: Charles Scribner's

Sons, 1958), p. 52. This view may well fit the position of enlightened self-interest discussed above, but not a true craft ethic.

7. The above remarks can be found in Thorstein Veblen, *The Instincts of Workmanship, and the State of the Industrial Arts* (New York: Sentry Press, reprinted 1964).

8. Veblen, pp. 348–349.

9. Graham Bannock, *The Juggernauts: The Age of the Big Corporation* (Harmondsworth, England: Penguin Books, 1973), p. 67.

10. Tom Peters, *Thriving on Chaos: Handbook for A Management Revolution* (New York: Alfred A. Knoff, 1988), p. 66.

11. Peters, p. 68.

12. Peters, pp. 69–70.

13. Peters, p. 84. Hayashi agrees that the Japanese have a strong affinity for craftsmanship. He says, "Japanese take pains with the hidden places, and they like to make fixtures attractive. Partly this is because customers demand it, but it is also because the worker, be he a blue-collar factory hand or an artisan, enjoys finishing a task properly. Difficult as many readers may find this to accept, such pride in a job well done—call it craftsmanship or perfectionism—is a major force in organizational and business activity in Japan." Shuji Hayashi, *Culture and Management in Japan*, trans. Frank Baldwin (Tokyo: University of Tokyo Press, 1988), p. 151. He suggests that this concern for craftsmanship is related to their strong aesthetic sense.

14. Drucker's views can be found in Peter F. Drucker, *Innovation and Entrepreneurship: Practice and Principles* (New York: Harper and Row, 1985).

APPENDIX I

IS A MORAL ORGANIZATION POSSIBLE?

1. The Pessimism Concerning Business Ethics: An Evaluation of the Popular View

Textbooks in business ethics often discuss, or at least mention, the popular notion that business is amoral or, at worst, immoral. People who have not thought much about values often hold contradictory views, as Socrates so effectively showed. Thus, Richard T. De George argues that if it is an accepted fact that business is amoral, why are people shocked and upset about business scandals; clearly, there are many people who, if they were consistent, would have to say that business-people at least should behave morally. Environmentalists and consumer groups believe this to be true, and a number of high ranking businesspeople would like to improve the morality, and not just the image, of business.[1] Since business is a part of society, it should be and is subjected to society's rules. But many business-people, De George argues, mistakenly believe that they have fulfilled their obligations, if their actions are lawful. "The law prohibits theft, enforces contracts, sets limits to advertising, and reinforces many moral norms."[2] He is clearly correct when he argues that although it is "convenient and easy" for businesspeople to equate legal and moral obligations, they are not the same.[3] Moreover, as Norman Bowie and others have mentioned, business practice is possible only if "business adheres to a minimum standard of justice and gives recognition to the rights of those engaged in the practice of business."[4] Applying Kant's categorical imperative (see Chapter 1), Bowie shows that such immoral actions as cheating, lying, and breaking agreements or promises are institutionally self-defeating.[5] Similarly, theft, fraud, kickbacks, and bribery undermine business practice. To attempt to make oneself an exception to rules is to act unjustly.

Much of the popular pessimism about business morality is, apparently, based upon the view that the goal of business is profit maximization. It is argued that because of this, business neglects people and, therefore, acts amorally and, at times, immorally. Before one can even begin to discuss this issue, a distinction should be made between the following questions: What is the goal of business? What is the motivation(s) of the businessperson? One should also distinguish between a description of business practices and an analysis of how business ought to behave from a moral point of view.

It may be a fact that many businesspeople believe that the goal of business is to maximize profit, but it is not clear that this should be the goal of business. In Chapter 6, we saw that Drucker argues that the purpose of business is to supply the wants and needs of customers, i.e., its goal should be better and more economic goods and services.[6] Of course, profit is essential to business, but Drucker maintains that this is because it is the basic test of the performance of a business, and it places a limit on what a business can do. What is called profit in the short run turns out to be something that pays for the cost of doing business in the longer run (it determines what a business can do). An emphasis on short term profit can create a conflict between social responsibility and business goals, but only profit can secure the future of business and allow it to make a social contribution as well as meet possible social obligations, e.g., supply more and better jobs, secure or increase the quality of a product, and pay for certain of society's services.

Although Drucker's position is controversial, some arguments can be used in its defense. Business, as the motto of the Harvard Business School tells us, wants to be considered a profession. Plato, in the *Republic*, shows that moneymaking is not a defining characteristic of professions. Every professional has some sort of knowledge or skill, and this knowledge, by the definition of a profession (as mentioned in Chapter 6), is directed toward someone or something other than the benefit of the professional. That is why professionals want to and deserve to get paid; they give services. Generally, every institutionalized profession exists for the sake of serving society. Thus, Drucker can dialectically refute the businessperson who wants to be considered a professional but also wants to define the goal of business as maximizing profit. Moreover, as De George says, "Business is a social enterprise. Its mandate and limits are both set by society."[7] If a business is so concerned with maximizing profit that it acts in a socially irresponsible way, society must deem such a purpose illegitimate, even if business management posits this goal. If business receives its mandate from society, it must be because society views it as an institution that provides people with desirable material goods and services and thus we are back to Drucker's position.

Concerning the motivation(s) of upper echelon businesspeople, it is unclear that their motives are any more materialistic than the average person's motives.[8] If managers today are professional managers, rather than owners, it is unclear, apart from the pressure in certain firms to maximize profits, that this would be the goal of such people who are paid according to scale, and who do not, themselves, get the profits. Moreover, as Galbraith argues, at the upper echelons of management, identification (identification with the goals of the firm) and adaptation (pursuit of corporate goals in order to accommodate these goals to one's preferences) are basic motives.[9] Growth is not necessarily a euphemism for profit; it provides managers with a higher purpose. Finally, I would argue that self-fulfillment or self-development is also a motive for upper level businesspeople.

In one important way materialism has been associated with American business because it has traditionally viewed itself as an economic institution. It is primarily because of this, that the so-called profit motive has played an important role in the traditional businessperson's view of business. But if business continues to view itself as a purely economic, rather than a social and a quasi-political, institution, as I suggested in Chapter 5, it can only continue to perpetuate the image of itself as an amoral, and possibly an immoral, institution. Moreover, this image will be reinforced if upper echelon managers of firms are narrow-minded financiers. Bottom line problems are easier to solve than ethical, or more generally qualitative, problems; but by ignoring such problems, a firm can readily become unjust through ignorance rather than evil intent.

If it is basically this narrow view of business that gives it a bad name from a moral standpoint, business, as an institution, need not be branded as amoral and certainly should not be considered immoral. However, as we have seen, concentrating on the basic values of American business has the advantage of emphasizing the source of American business character models, and by considering these, we can best determine historically the morality or lack of it in American business. In Chapters 2 and 3, I have shown that such basic American business character models as the Protestant, frontier, robber baron, and organization man ethics leave something to be desired from a moral point of view.

2. Is a Formal Moral Organization Possible? A Discussion of Alternative Philosophical Views

If the subject of business ethics cannot be undermined by the more usual or popular type of pessimism, possibly one can object to it on a more abstract level. Moral language properly applies to people; one may argue, therefore, that persons and corporations are not analogous enough to apply such language to corporations correctly. But this has been denied by some philosophers, the most discussed of whom is Peter French.

French argues that corporations which have a CID (Corporate Internal Decision Structure) can synthesize "the decisions and acts of various human beings and other intentional systems into a corporate action."[10] They are "Davidsonian agents"; some of the things they do can be described in terms of intentionality. Davidsonian agents, as moral agents, must conform to "the Extended Principle of Accountability" (EPA)—accountability "extends" to deliberate nonintentional actions—and "the Principle of Responsive Adjustment" (PRA)—a person should be held responsible for previous unintentional actions, "if he or she subsequently unintentionally acts in ways that are likely to cause repetitions of the untoward outcome."[11] In the above sense, corporations, which have a CID and are capable of "non-programmed decision making," are able to function in a manner analogous to a moral person.[12] Since corporations and persons can function analogously, corporations are morally responsible for their actions. French's intention is "to provide persuasive metaphysical and moral reasons for treating certain kinds of corporations as members in full standing of the moral community."[13] These corporations are not "mere machines."[14]

Some philosophers believe that although there are certain similarities between formal organizations such as corporations and persons, the dissimilarities are too great to support French's position. For example, Thomas Donaldson and De George argue that corporations do not have natural rights, but persons do.[15] Moreover, they argue that corporations are only "juristic persons" or creatures of the law.[16] Donaldson questions whether French's emphasis on intentionality is sufficient for determining a moral agent. De George agrees with Donaldson that it is wrong to treat corporations as moral persons because of the basic disanalogies between corporations and persons. He argues that human beings, as ends in themselves, have moral worth; corporations are mere instrumentalities and, as such, have no moral worth. Moreover, "human beings, being ends in themselves, have many general obligations that cannot apply to corporations. The rules of charity, concern for one's fellow human beings, and so on are inapplicable to corporations."[17] Human beings have "emotive capacities"; they are capable of feeling moral blame and shame, but corporations cannot. Since morality entails emotive capacity, he argues, we have a good reason for denying "moral personhood" to corporations. He agrees with Donaldson, therefore, that intentionality is not a sufficient condition for "moral personhood."[18] Moreover, Donaldson sides with De George in arguing that corporations cannot, necessarily, be considered moral persons because they may lack a heart; they may be incapable of sympathy.

I agree with De George and Donaldson that formal organizations and persons are not analogous enough to attribute natural rights to corporations. Nor do they have intrinsic value in the sense that human beings do. However, De George and others argue that one does not have to make corporations moral persons to hold them responsible for their actions. De George argues that since corporations are used by human beings for certain ends, they can be considered "moral actors" and, as such, can be morally evaluated.[19] Larry May argues, and others agree, that corporate responsibility is a type of collective responsibility. "The high ranking managers work through an already existing decision-making process which allows these individuals to reach joint decisions under the name of the corporation."[20] As De George says, we talk about collectives acting morally or immorally; whether a collective has a CID structure is irrelevant from the standpoint of moral judgment. Since corporations can be "moral actors," the responsibility for their actions are "traceable to human beings either individually or collectively."[21] A corporation cannot act unless people act through it, and people are morally responsible for what they do. Although corporations have both moral and legal responsibilities, he thinks that they should be considered legal, rather than moral, persons.[22]

De George seems to be correct in arguing, against French, that corporations do not have to be moral persons to hold them responsible for their actions. But De George is able to refute French, in part, because French's strong position on the analogy between corporations and persons is unnecessary for the view he is defending. I would think that a basic reason for defending the "moral personhood" theory of corporations is to show that formal organizations can function like a moral person. That is, besides having a CID, they potentially have something analogous to character which can be evaluated as virtuous or vicious. Moreover, one can evaluate whether they are trustworthy. Because of this, it is surprising to find that French does not consider this issue. He says, "I am not concerned with why the corporation should be moral."[23] But if this fuller notion of corporate personhood cannot be defended, is business ethics, as a viable field, possible?

From the standpoint of the possibility of business ethics, a serious challenge to the position (expressed above) of De George and Donaldson can be mounted. Even if we can hold corporations responsible for actions determined by decisions made by corporate officials who act in the name of the corporation, it may not be realistic to treat corporations as moral agents; this would be the case if corporations function in an amoral manner, and can only be made responsible for their actions by the threat of some external force, e.g., legal or public pressure. I think that De George and Donaldson are correct in arguing, against French, that intentionality is insufficient for determining moral personhood. But it is unclear that they are correct in arguing that formal organizations and persons are not analogous enough to attribute "emotive capacities" or "heart" to corporations, although the related attributes are necessary for moral personhood. Moreover, aside from the problem of the correctness of their position, it is important to understand what is at stake in emphasizing the dissimilarities between corporations and persons. If the dissimilarities are sufficient to deny a concept analogous to moral personhood to formal organizations, then it is unclear in what sense corporations can function in a moral, as opposed to a merely legal, fashion. Although we may be able to hold corporations morally responsible for their actions, this need not entail anything more than the use of nonmoral modes of societal persuasion, e.g., legal or public pressure. Such a view of corporate responsibility is quite different from one which conceives of corporations as true moral agents; that is, corporations are capable of organizing for moral as well as economic purposes.

De George correctly emphasizes that one should distinguish among the different types of responsibility that can pertain to a corporation, i.e., corporate, legal, social, and moral responsibility.[24] Business ethics should be concerned with moral responsibility, e.g., corporate moral responsibility. We have seen that De George argues that corporations are moral actors, but not moral persons. Possibly, because of this he argues for what may be called a minimalist view of corporate moral responsibility. He suggests that corporations are obligated to obey "the moral law," but, specifically, they are morally obligated to avoid deliberate harm. However, since he believes that corporations are not ends in themselves, they are not morally obligated to develop in any specific way. Nor is it very helpful, he thinks, to apply terms like "virtue" and "character" to corporations. Given this position, however, corporate moral responsibility is considerably watered down, and it is closely allied with the other three notions of corporate responsibility. That is, corporate responsibility is determined by the nature of the corporation, and since it is not a true moral agent, it will function morally under legal and social restrictions. Therefore, it is tempting to argue, as I have suggested, that corporations will function, when they can, as amoral institutions and will meet their moral obligations when legal and public pressures are considered threatening enough.

Kenneth E. Goodpaster and John B. Matthews suggest that, in a primary sense, we call a person morally responsible if he or she is trustworthy or reliable.[25] Since they develop a close analogy between corporations and persons, they can maintain that corporations can be morally responsible, in their sense, but it is debatable whether De George's position allows this to be possible. No wonder he must water down the notion of moral responsibility as it applies to formal organizations; it must be made to fit his view of the corporation. It is, therefore, important to examine the position of Goodpaster and Matthews and determine whether it is a viable theory.

Goodpaster and Matthews disagree with Donaldson, De George, and other thinkers holding similar views in not only supporting French's general position, but also in going further by maintaining, as they put it, that corporations can have a conscience and, indeed, "a heart." "Organizational agents such as corporations should be no more and no less morally responsible (rational, self-interested, altruistic) than ordinary persons."[26] Using William Frankena's position, they isolate two essential traits of moral responsibility: Rationality ("rational decision-making, that is, lack of impulsiveness, care in mapping out alternatives and consequences, clarity about goals and purposes, attention to details of implementation") and respect (concern for the effects of one's actions and respect for others in the sense of "taking their needs and interests seriously").[27] Both of these features can apply to corporations. They agree with French that rationality or the lack of it can be attributed to the "internal decision structure" of an organization. Also, features related to respect have been built into the managerial systems of some corporations; these firms have institutionalized concern for employees, consumers, and the public. Not only can an organization have or lack character, but also a corporation can develop in moral stages just as people do.

Given the position of Goodpaster and Matthews, it is not surprising that they admit a debt to Plato. More specifically, they maintain that their method is an inversion of the one used in the *Republic* (justice in the state is a model for determining justice in the individual). They call such a method a type of projection; one should determine the processes associated with personal moral responsibility and project them to the level of organizations.[28]

An understanding of Plato's method, I believe, requires more attention than has been given to it by Goodpaster and Matthews. It might be helpful, then, in analyzing this method, to consider the way in which Plato uses it in the *Republic*.[29] Plato, in a sense, does project the virtues of the Republic's citizens to the city, but the virtues of these people are not identical to the virtues of the city. Indeed, Plato does not say that the city and the human soul are identical; he says that justice in the city and justice in the individual are identical, but all the city's virtues are not necessarily identical to all the individual's virtues.

There is an obvious sense in which the three classes of the city do not parallel the three capacities of the human soul. Even if, as Plato says, one class is dominantly appetite, a second, spirit, and a third, reason, each class is composed of human beings and is, therefore, more complex than the corresponding class capacity. Each member of a class has a tripartite soul and can partake, in some sense and in some degree, of the four cardinal virtues (wisdom, courage, temperance, and justice). But each capacity of the soul is evidently not tripartite. Moreover, the city abstracts from individual capacities; a specific virtue in the city is not necessarily identical to the corresponding virtue of an individual. Reason not only functions in an organizational capacity, it has its own peculiar desire, which is essential to it, the desire for the truth. Reason in the city is derived from the philosopher, but the state abstracts from reason's peculiar drive (*hormē*). Similarly, the proper development of the spirited element in people entails a type of military and administrative courage which finds its parallel in the city (spirit sides with reason against unreasonable appetites), but the nature of a person's courage is dependent upon the degree of the person's rationality. Thus, the courage of a philosopher-king is not the courage of an Auxiliary. Moreover, the distinctive goals of spirit, honor, victory, and the quality of aggressiveness or, at least, assertiveness are different in the above two types of people. The virtuous city, then, is not the virtuous person writ large, and Plato's argument has more validity if it is taken to mean that there are important parallels between virtue in the city and virtue in the individual. What Plato's argument does show is that in spite of the lack of identity between his city and the soul of the individual, there is enough similarity to structure a city properly by organizing people with the requisite virtues to function in roles for which they are suited. In this way, one may hope for a proper compromise between a virtuous or psychically healthy city and virtuous or psychically healthy citizens. In a broad sense, the morality of the city is derived from the character of its citizens, but the city is moral only if the virtues of its citizens are properly developed and organized. A moral organization is a result of good management. We have seen that, for Plato, justice provides the city with a proper coherence; each person is able to fulfill basic capacities (but not without compromises), while contributing in some necessary way to the common good. This requires that the rulers are wise in a philosophical sense; the rulers have knowledge of the whole and can organize the city in the interest of the whole. The citizens must be temperate or moderate in the sense of being satisfied with their place in the city, and the aggressive and competitive (spirited) types in the city must be guided by those people who are truly wise.

In Chapter 5, I mentioned the theory of corporate social responsibility called the managerial creed. The managerial creed maintains that managers are not merely responsible to shareholders; they should justly or fairly balance the legitimate, though often competing, claims of customers, employees, suppliers, and the general public, as well as shareholders. The emphasis is on both a grasp of the whole and on managerial ethics. I suggested that this position is Platonic; that is, business statesmanship, like political statesmanship, necessitates both knowledge of an organized whole and sound moral as well as economic leadership. Such managers must appeal to some criterion of justice or fairness in balancing or mediating among the interests of those segments of the population which are seen to be substantially affected by the activities of the firm. I suggested that, ethically, as applied to modern corporate business, this view is sounder than the classical view.

We saw that in the 1980's, management theories that are more in accord with the managerial creed than with the classical position have been developed by such management theorists as Ouchi (*Theory Z*), Pascale and Athos (*The Art of Japanese Management*), and Peters and Waterman (*In Search of Excellence*).[30] In general, "excellent companies" (to use Peters and Waterman's term) are people-oriented. They create environments in which employees can develop their abilities and be treated with respect and dignity, consumers can get quality products and services, and shareholders can do well because such firms do well. In such companies, management functions well, for the entire firm is productive.

It is reasonable to assume, then, that some contemporary management theorists would not be adverse to the position of Goodpaster and Matthews which, in the words of French, treat corporations as "members in full standing of the moral community" rather than as "mere machines." However, one should not be surprised to find the diametrically opposed position, a view more in accord with the classical position, maintained by competent philosophers. Such a philosopher is John Ladd.

Ladd argues that formal organizations (bureaucracies) are best understood on the analogy of the machine. Given the logic of formal organizations,

> the sole standard for the evaluation of an organization, its
> activities and its decisions, is its effectiveness in achieving its
> objectives.... This kind of effectiveness is called 'rationality'.

Thus rationality is defined in terms of the category of means and ends.[31]

Formal organizations emphasize "the autonomy of the activity and the immunity of the rules governing the game."[32] Decisions made by officials of an organization are made impersonally in the name of the organization and aim at implementing the "objectives of the organization." This, he maintains, is "the theory of organizational decision-making."[33] "The logical function of the goal in the organizational language-game is to supply the value premises to be used in making decisions, justifying and evaluating them."[34] Decisions and actions of corporate officers unrelated to their goals are to be construed as actions of individuals rather than of the organization. Since corporate rationality properly pertains to determining means and not ends (the ends justify the means), moral judgments, strictly speaking, do not pertain to corporate decisions. Of course, generally accepted moral views of, for example, a society will be considered in making corporate judgments, but this is the case only because they are pertinent to determining means to goals. Therefore, corporations and persons are governed by different moral principles; corporate ethics are determined by corporate goals.

> Thus, for logical reasons it is improper to expect organizational conduct to conform to the ordinary principles of morality. We cannot and must not expect formal organizations, or their representatives acting in their official capacities, to be honest, courageous, considerate, sympathetic, or to have any kind of moral integrity. Such concepts are not in the vocabulary...of the organizational language-game.[35]

Corporate actions are subject to the standard of "rational efficiency (utility)" while "individuals...are subject to the ordinary standards of morality."[36] Corporate people, then, function according to a double standard—amorally as officials of an organization and morally as private persons. In this way, espionage, deception, and lying can be justified as rational insofar as they serve corporate ends.

Although formal organizations are not moral persons, and thus have no rights or moral responsibilities, persons in a corporation do have rights. How, then, can justice exist in a corporation? Ladd gives the obvious answer. Since a formal organization is an amoral machine in which the end justifies the means, "it follows that the only way to make the rights and interests of individuals...logically relevant to organizational decision-making is to convert them into pressures of one sort or another, e.g., to bring the pressure of the law or of public opinion to bear on the organization. Such pressures would then be introduced into the rational decision-making as limiting operating conditions."[37] However, he thinks that there is a kind of alienation that is a logical result of the nature of formal organizations, and he is properly concerned with this. Since our society is highly organized, many people are forced to live according to the double standard mentioned above. Moreover, the more we immerse ourselves in "social actions," the more we tend to use amoral rather than moral social standards as a basis for decisions and evaluations of actions.[38] The administrator's point of view breeds alienation (from people and moral decisions); the moral point of view is essentially people-oriented.

The avoidance of an exclusive either/or between formal organizations and persons is a basic human dilemma of our age. We have seen that Ladd takes a realistic view of formal organizations. Within its "language-game" moral evaluations are irrelevant. One may attempt, from the outside, to evaluate the morality of the goals and, generally, the actions of organizations, but these evaluations, as such, will have no effect on the formal organization. "When we speak of the responsibility of corporations," he says, "we are dealing with questions of social control: how can the conduct of corporations be brought into conformity with the demands of morality."[39] Corporations are motivated by self-interest, and thus sanctions should be used to bring them into line.

Goodpaster and Matthews understand that Ladd's position, which they agree is supported by people both inside and outside of business, "represents a tremendous barrier to the development of business ethics both as a field of inquiry and as a practical force in managerial decision making."[40] In evaluating Ladd's position, one must be careful, as a business ethics "specialist," that one does not rationalize (in the pejorative sense) one's own position. They raise the question of whether or not the projection of moral attributes to organizations is advisable. They consider two traditional alternative frames of reference for corporate responsibility, "the invisible hand" and "the hand of government." "Both views," they suggest, "reject the exercise of independent moral judgment by corporations as actors in society. Neither view trusts corporate leaders with stewardship over what are often called noneconomic values."[41] Thus, like Ladd, people who hold the above positions "locate moral restraint in forces external to the person and the corporation."[42] These thinkers are more pessimistic than Goodpaster and Matthews about the possibility of a moral corporation and this, apparently, is the basic disagreement. One should note, however, that Goodpaster and Matthews are not naive; they recognize that their view is not a part of the "received wisdom," and "the imperatives of ethics cannot be relied on—nor have they ever been relied on—without a context of external sanctions."[43]

3. A Discussion of the Skepticism Concerning the Possibility of a Platonic Moral Organization

One may argue that Ladd's position, on the one hand, and the positions of French, Goodpaster, and Matthews, on the other, represent extreme views, and the truth lies somewhere in the middle. This appears to be the view of De George and Donaldson. Virginia Held clearly attempts to steer between what she considers the extreme views of Ladd and French. She argues that Ladd's view of a formal organization—that it is like a machine—and French's position—the corporation is a "full-fledged moral person"—are untenable.[44] On the surface, it would appear to be reasonable to steer a middle course between the above extremes, but such a position becomes more doubtful, or at least more difficult, if we consider the problem in the broader context of the history of political philosophy.

It is important for Plato to develop a close parallel between the city and the human soul, for he can then argue for a parallel between the virtue or psychic health of the city and the individual. If this is accepted, it is reasonable to posit a harmony between the good of the city and the good of the citizens. But the Platonic position is not feasible if people are motivated principally by narrow self-interest. If this is true, as many businesspeople believe, then Plato would insist that an organization will not be an harmonious whole; indeed, it will be saturated with injustice.[45] In this context, it might be possible for an individual to be just, but more improbable that an organization would be just.

One could trace the above problem to issues implicit in the early stages of developing the ideal city of the *Republic*. Within the context of economic values, the initial healthy community, discussed by Socrates, is just because each person has simple needs and is an artisan. If each person is an artisan and works for his or her own advantage, given a system of exchange, the good of the whole will be served, and each artisan will derive satisfaction and, possibly, a sense of pride from his or her work. But not only is such a community not satisfying insofar as it does not provide for the fulfillment of a person's higher needs—spirited and intellectual needs—it will not be materialistic enough for people with Glaucon's "need" for luxuries. Under such an impetus, Socrates' initial community would be destroyed by the desire for wealth or material possessions, and a more luxurious city would take its place. The ideal of this luxurious city would be maximizing profits. In such a community, the value of being an artisan, either from the standpoint of the common good or from the good of the individual (the satisfaction, pride in accomplishment, and sense of personal dignity that results from craftsmanship) will be minimized, for the lucrative "arts" will be most emphasized. Injustice will be one consequence of the resulting conflicts among people. Platonic justice would be impossible because people will not necessarily do what they are most suited for and, generally, the common good will not be served.

A fundamental question for the Platonic approach is whether human beings, by nature, are capable of organizing a community based upon virtue or are narrowly self-interested goals the most we can expect from the great majority of people. According to the political philosopher Leo Strauss, how we answer this question will determine whether we will side with the classical or the modern solution in political theory. "It was possible," says Strauss, "to speak of the classical solution to the problem of political philosophy because there is a fundamental and at the same time specific agreement among all classical political philosophers: the goal of political life is virtue, and the order most conducive to virtue is the aristocratic republic, or else the mixed regime."[46] Strauss suggests that modern political philosophies differ from classical political philosophy in maintaining that such a view is unrealistic; the founder of this movement was Machiavelli. According to Strauss, Machiavelli believes that what is fundamentally wrong with classical political philosophy is that it makes virtue the basis of the "best regime," but such a regime would probably never exist. In political theory, therefore, we should be guided by realistic objectives, by what human beings do in societies and not what they ought to do. By lowering our standards, we increase the probability of actualizing our position. For Machiavelli, according to Strauss, "virtue is nothing but civic virtue, patriotism or devotion to collective selfishness."[47] Arguing in a Machiavellian manner, Strauss says,

> You want justice? I am going to show you how you can get it.... You will get it only by making injustice utterly unprofitable. What you need is not so much formation of character and moral appeal, as the right kind of institutions, institutions with teeth in them.[48]

This is essentially Ladd's position. As it develops in political philosophy, it is more familiarly associated with Thomas Hobbes. Strauss argues that Hobbes developed the tradition that classical political philosophy aimed too high. Natural right, so essential according to Donaldson and De George in distinguishing persons from formal organizations, is derived from our basic selfish drives, the most fundamental of which is self-preservation. Civil society is based upon fear, and established governments expand the desire for self-preservation into "comfortable self-preservation."[49] Materialism, not justice or virtue (human excellence), is our goal, and power is the means of securing it. If anything, John Locke stressed materialism more by emphasizing property. Strauss says that Locke's "amoral substitute for morality" is acquisitiveness.[50]

If people are basically motivated by narrow self-interest, the classical virtues cannot exist within an organization, except as mere shams of virtue. For example, temperance is reduced to obedience, loyalty, docility, and concern for security; that is, the values of the organization man. Courage degenerates into the excessive cutthroat competitiveness, brutality (power mongering), and emphasis on personal fame or glory of the robber baron type of corporate official. Wisdom also is degraded; it becomes the narrow cleverness of the person who can find the so-called practical solutions to immediate, concrete problems (especially as related to material concerns). Finally, justice becomes, as Glaucon (in the *Republic*) says, a necessary evil; it is determined by what is lawful and enforced by power. It is to one's personal advantage, then, to seize power and manipulate laws for one's own benefit. Indeed, one is successful when he or she can be unjust (in a big way) while appearing just. The rest of the people must settle for the stability or security, which may be illusory, that is provided by the laws. (Glaucon's position is, unfortunately, too readily accepted by many businesspeople.) If this is the case, one would suspect an analogous situation to occur in organizations. That is, there is a strong tendency for people in power to use that power for their own advantage, while less powerful members of a firm gain whatever security and material advantages they can. The result of this argument is that within the context of what Strauss would call the Machiavellian society—in our case, the formal organization—business ethics, as Goodpaster and Matthews warn us, "both as a field of inquiry and as a practical force in managerial decision making" is improbable.

Reinhold Niebuhr, in *Moral Man and Immoral Society*, develops the type of challenge that philosophers who hold a position similar to that of Goodpaster and Matthews must face squarely. We have seen that Goodpaster and Matthews consider two traits that they maintain are essential to moral responsibility—rationality and respect. Niebuhr raises questions about the adequacy of both of these traits in the context of organizational behavior. He argues that "since the ultimate sources of social conflicts and injustice are to be found in the ignorance and selfishness of men, it is natural that the hope of establishing justice by increasing human intelligence and benevolence should be perennially renewed."[51] This clearly pertains to the position of Goodpaster and Matthews. Against this, he argues that "men will never be wholly reasonable, and the proportion of reason to impulse becomes increasingly negative when we proceed from the life of the individual to that of social groups."[52] Moreover, the "obligation to achieve social objectives" is weak when such goals conflict with "the possessive instinct or the will-to-power."[53] In his introduction, Niebuhr again questions the adequacy of the above two traits. The morality of groups is inferior to that of individuals because: (1) The rationality of groups is insufficient to cope with "the natural impulses by which society achieves its cohesion."[54] (2) The force of "collective egoism" is so much greater than that of individual egoism that the only way in which it can be prevented from exploiting weakness is to control it with the use of power. He argues against the more optimistic psychologists, sociologists, philosophers, educators, and religious idealists who believe that people's egoism, functioning collectively, can be controlled by the development of rationality and goodwill. They do not understand "the power of self-interest and collective egoism in all intergroup relations," and that in groups, reason is often the servant of prejudice and passion, and thus "social conflict [is] an inevitability in human history."[55] The Ladd thesis, and its consequent pessimism about business morality, is highlighted in Niebuhr's emphasis on the power of collective self-interest.

> The more the moral problem is shifted from the relations of individuals to the relations of groups and collectives, the more the preponderance of the egotistic impulses over the social ones is established. It is therefore revealed that no inner checks are powerful enough to bring them under control. Social control must consequently be attempted.[56]

Niebuhr believes that it is difficult to take a middle of the road position. The danger of political realism, he suggests, is that it entails perpetual societal conflict. Social stability necessitates the use of coercion which leads to social injustice, the undermining of which requires further coercion. "If power is needed to destroy power, how is this new power to be made ethical?"[57] But the moralist can be as dangerous as the political realist. He often fails to recognize the more subtle, covert forms of coercion, and accepts "a too uncritical glorification of co-operation and mutuality."[58] His considered position is that political realism must be tempered by the idealism of the moral person, but this idealism, in turn, must be tempered by "the realities of man's collective life."[59] But given Niebuhr's conception of these "realities," it is difficult to comprehend how a moral organization is possible. Nonetheless, as we have seen, Chapter 6 is based on the premise that the obstacles to creating a Platonic type of business organization are not insurmountable.

One would hope, for the sake of business ethics, that a Platonic type of solution is viable; or some solution can be found that is close enough to this position to allow justice, and virtue in general, to function in formal organizations in a manner other than the degenerate form described above. My conception of a Platonic type of business organization is a more optimistic alternative to (what I think are) overly pessimistic Machiavellian and Hobbesian theories of the corporation such as Ladd's. Similarly, my theory attempts to counter Niebuhr's pessimistic view; namely, human ignorance and selfishness must necessarily be intensified, rather than moderated, in organizational life. I have argued that Platonic virtue is possible for business organizations. This thesis is based upon the belief that Platonic business statesmanship (business wisdom) and a Platonic type of business virtue that is compatible with self-interest (in the broad sense discussed in Chapter 6 rather than in a narrow sense—selfishness) are possible.

NOTES

1. Richard T. De George, *Business Ethics* (New York: Macmillan, 1982), p. 5.

2. De George, p. 8.

3. De George, pp. 8–9.

4. Norman Bowie, *Business Ethics* (Englewood Cliffs, New Jersey: Prentice Hall, 1982), p. 39.

5. Bowie, pp. 41–43.

6. See n. 22, Chapter 6.

7. De George, p. 8.

8. Milton Friedman is a popular exponent of the view that people's basic incentive is the profit motive. See, for example, Milton and Rose Friedman, *Free to Choose* (New York: Avon Books, 1979), p. 15.

9. John K. Galbraith, *The New Industrial State* (New York: Signet Books, 1967), pp. 141–143, 162–168.

10. Peter French, "Principles of Responsibility, Shame, and the Corporation," in *Shame, Responsibility and the Corporation*, ed. Hugh Curlter (New York: Haven, 1986), p. 22.

11. French, p. 34.

12. French, p. 37.

13. French, p. 48.

14. French, p. 48.

15. Thomas Donaldson, "Personalizing Corporate Ontology: The French Way," in *Shame, Responsibility and the Corporation*, ed. Hugh Curlter (New York: Haven, 1986), p. 104. Richard T. De George, "Corporations and Morality," in *Shame, Responsibility and the Corporation*, ed. Hugh Curlter (New York: Haven, 1986), pp. 61–62. Cf. John Ladd, "Persons and Responsibility: Ethical Concepts and

Impertinent Analogies," in *Shame, Responsibility and the Corporation*, ed. Hugh Curlter (New York: Haven, 1986), p. 86.

16. Donaldson, p. 106. Cf. De George, "Corporations and Morality," p. 60.

17. De George, "Corporations and Morality," p. 62.

18. De George, "Corporations and Morality," p. 62.

19. De George, "Corporations and Morality," p. 63.

20. Larry May, "Negligence and Corporate Criminality," in *Shame, Responsibility and the Corporation*, ed. Hugh Curlter (New York: Haven, 1986), p. 141.

21. De George, "Corporations and Morality," p. 64.

22. De George does recognize the possibility of situations arising in which the ascription of responsibility to an individual or individuals in a corporation is difficult or impossible even though the corporation was the cause of the immoral action. In this case, he thinks that one should change the decision structure. But Goodpaster and Matthews correctly argue that corporate moral responsibility is not reducible to responsibilities of individuals in business. This type of reductionism does not take into account the notion that the whole is not the sum of its parts. "Intelligence needs to be structured, organized, divided, and recombined in complex processes for complex purposes." Kenneth E. Goodpaster and John B. Matthews, Jr., "Can a Corporation Have a Conscience?" in *Ethical Issues in Business: A Philosophical Approach*, eds. Thomas Donaldson and Patricia H. Werhane, 3rd ed. (Englewood Cliffs, New Jersey: Prentice-Hall, 1988), p. 148. Social responsibility, itself, must be managed.

23. French, p. 38.

24. De George distinguishes different types of responsibilities that pertain to corporations. Corporate responsibility is determined by corporate goals and the interests of owners and employees. Corporations are legal creations; they "have only those characteristics granted by law" (De George, "Corporations and Morality," pp. 68–69), and they are obligated, like other organizations, to function within the laws of a society. The term "social responsibilities of corporations" can be used in the broad sense to include all corporate related responsibilities—corporate, legal, and moral—but, in a narrow sense, the term refers to societal demands imposed on corporations.

25. Goodpaster and Matthews, p. 141.

26. Goodpaster and Matthews, p. 141.

27. Goodpaster and Matthews, p. 142.

28. There is a sense in which the virtues of the state in the *Republic* are derived from the virtues of the people in the state (See *Republic* 435e–436a). The capacities and corresponding virtues of the state are derived from the capacities and corresponding virtues of the people. Constitutions are derived from "the characters of the citizens" (*Republic* 544d). Thus, a state reflects the character of its citizens.

29. The reader may recall that I provide a simplified analysis of Plato's discussion of the human soul and the virtues in the section in Chapter 5 entitled, "Plato on the Human Soul and the Cardinal Virtues."

30. William G. Ouchi, *Theory Z: How American Business Can Meet the Japanese Challenge* (Reading, Mass.: Addison-Wesley, 1981). Richard T. Pascale and Anthony G. Athos, *The Art of Japanese Management: Applications for American Executives* (New York: Warner Books, 1981). Thomas J. Peters and Robert H. Waterman Jr. *In Search of Excellence: Lessons from America's Best-Run Companies* (New York: Harper and Row, 1982).

31. John Ladd, "Morality and the Ideal of Rationality in Formal Organizations," in *Ethical Issues in Business: A Philosophical Approach*, eds. Thomas Donaldson and Patricia H. Werhane, 3rd ed. (Englewood Cliffs, New Jersey: Prentice-Hall), p. 114.

32. Ladd, p. 111.

33. Ladd, p. 112.

34. Ladd, p. 113.

35. Ladd, p. 116.

36. Ladd, p. 116.

37. Ladd, p. 119.

38. Ladd, p. 120.

39. Ladd, "Persons and Responsibility," p. 93.

40. Goodpaster and Matthews, pp. 140–141.

41. Goodpaster and Matthews, p. 145.

42. Goodpaster and Matthews, p. 146.

43. Goodpaster and Matthews, p. 148.

44. Virginia Held, "Corporations, Persons, and Responsibility," in *Shame, Responsibility and the Corporation*, ed. Hugh Curlter (New York: Haven, 1986), pp. 161–181.

45. Kristol points out that capitalism promises three things: continued development of materialism, freedom for its citizens, and a just society. He argues that, in contrast to the Aristotelian ideal of creating a "high and memorable civilization," capitalism "lowered its sights." Moreover, although capitalism promised a just society, the passion for affluence and liberty subverted the promise of a virtuous life. Irving Kristol, *Two Cheers for Capitalism* (New York: Mentor Book, 1978), pp. 241–246.

46. Leo Strauss, "What is Political Philosophy," in *What is Political Philosophy and Other Studies* (Illinois: The Free Press of Glencoe, 1959), p. 40.

47. Strauss, p. 42.

48. Strauss, p. 43.

49. Strauss, p. 48.

50. Strauss, p. 49.

51. Reinhold Niebuhr, *Moral Man and Immoral Society: A Study in Ethics and Politics* (New York: Charles Scribner's Sons, 1960), p. 23.

52. Niebuhr, p. 35.

53. Niebuhr, p. 35.

54. Niebuhr, p. XII.

55. Niebuhr, p. XX.

56. Niebuhr, p. 262.

57. Niebuhr, p. 231.

58. Niebuhr, p. 233.

59. Niebuhr, p. 258.

APPENDIX II

CORPORATE CULTURE AND VIRTUE ETHICS

A corporate culture is defined in terms of the values that guide the corporation's conduct, and the culture is strong if these values are clearly visible and emphasized so that, as Terrence E. Deal and Allan A. Kennedy maintain, they give meaning and purpose to corporate activity.[1] It is often argued that business cultures reflect their environments in the sense that the specific realities of the marketplace are instrumental in molding specific corporate cultures. Deal and Kennedy say, "Each company faces a different reality in the marketplace depending on its products, competitors, customers, technologies, government influences and so on."[2] Instead of relying on mechanistic approaches—structures, systems, formalistic planning—to cope with economic changes and competitive pressures, the corporate culture approach is more philosophical; the basic values of a strong corporate culture guide its strategy and organization, and in a healthy firm, the daily beliefs follow from these guiding values.[3] The guiding values, if they are the real values of a firm rather than those paid lip service to, reflect the basic beliefs of top management. In firms in which putative values do not conform to daily values (generally because employees believe they constitute corporate image rather than substance), employees usually interpret them in a cynical manner. In strong corporate cultures, however, strong managerial leadership shapes the values of the firm, and these values flow down through its layers. They are reinforced by stories about heroes and legends, corporate rites, rituals and symbols, and a set of informal rules instantiated in employees' daily activities.

The belief that strong cultures can cope effectively with competitive pressures and economic changes seems to contradict the generally recognized fact that the habits of employees in strong corporate cultures make the culture highly resistant to change. Strong culture enthusiasts argue, however, that resistance to change in such cultures can be countered by building into a strong culture's customs an inclination for "flexibility and innovation."[4] In such firms, Charles O'Reilly argues, employees are trained in "constructive confrontation" (Intel) or "creative conflict" (J and J) which teaches them to deal effectively with conflict in constructive, rather than destructive, ways.[5] Although radical external changes that force a strong corporate culture to change core values are resisted by such cultures, they, nonetheless, have important features that allow them to cope with change more effectively than bureaucratic firms. Pascale argues that in such firms people are clearer about what is required because conduct is guided by known values. "Organizations that socialize effectively manage a lot of internal ambiguity. This tends to free up time and energy; more goes toward getting the job done and focusing on external things like competition and the consumer."[6] In weak culture firms, much of one's time and energy is spent in corporate politics, both in order to get anything done and to solidify one's position and to advance. Cooperation, integrity, and communication, he argues, thrive in strong, rather than weak, corporate cultures.

The ethical superiority of strong culture firms, according to their enthusiasts, is underscored by their people orientation.[7] Thus, Pascale and Athos agree with Thomas Watson of IBM that such basic values as respect for the individual rather than strategy is the essential factor in corporate success.

The corporate culture approach to management has been popular among management theorists in the 1980's. Since it is clearly an agent-oriented approach, it would seem that a virtue, rather than an action-based, ethic would be most helpful in doing business ethics in this context. I shall now consider this issue.

In his *Theory of the Moral life*, John Dewey correctly maintains that the term "ethics" is derived from the word "*ethos*" which originally meant customs (of a group) and later was associated with character. That which is moral first appears as customs, for these are habitual ways of acting approved by a group or society.[8] Thus, the ethics of a group is determined by its culture, and different corporate cultures have different ethics or modes of conduct. Such conduct is embedded, by conditioning, in employee habits. The essential habits are called virtues because they constitute the "excellences" that are thought to be necessary for the firm to flourish. It is important to understand that ethics, in this sense, is not reflective; it is what Dewey calls customary morality and is generally called conventional morality. Thus, what are considered virtues in a corporate culture may not, in a proper sense, be virtues. Dewey says,

> In customary morality, acts and traits of character are not esteemed because they are virtuous; rather they are virtues because they are supported by social approval and admiration. So virtue means valor in a martial society, and denotes enterprise, thrift, industriousness in an industrialized community.... Reflection tries to reverse the order: it wants to discover what *should* be esteemed so that approbation will follow what is decided to be *worth* approving, instead of designating virtues on the basis of what happens to be especially looked up to and rewarded in a particular society.[9]

If we take a reflective rather than a conventional point of view, we should consider what such a position on the nature of virtue should be. I believe that, in this regard, Platonic ideas discussed at the end of Chapter 1 are helpful. We saw that a basic premise regulating Socratic inquiry is the position that virtue is a good and, therefore, is always beneficial. Using this premise, Plato shows that external and internal goods are not necessarily beneficial unless they are guided by wisdom (*phronēsis*). Virtue in a proper sense, then, must be based upon wisdom; that is, traits which purport to be virtuous character traits can only be so if they are under the control of wisdom. Therefore, wisdom is necessary for a reflective morality in the best sense. A second point mentioned in Chapter 1, which, for Plato, follows from the above regulative premise, is also essential to the distinction between conventional and reflective morality. If virtue is always beneficial, a virtue is beneficial (a good) for both the possessor of the virtue and those who are affected by the virtuous conduct.

I shall apply this Deweyian and Platonic analysis to corporate cultures. Advocates of strong corporate cultures, such as Deal and Kennedy, at times betray the conventional, rather than reflective, nature of corporate virtue. We have seen that Deal and Kennedy argue that the realities of the marketplace mold specific corporate cultures. Corporate CEOs are successful if they can shape and mold corporate cultures to fit the "shifting needs of the marketplace."[10] But if business is fraught with such contingency, if its realm is the radically changeable, then the ethic of a strong corporate culture, and therefore the "virtues" that drive that ethic, is based upon a certain amount of illusion and manipulation.

In developing the above considerations, one might argue that the guiding values of a strong corporate culture are used to harness human energies, loyalties, needs for identifying with something praiseworthy, and the warm feelings of a community effort in a specific direction. But what of the disillusionment that comes when the contingent nature of these values are revealed by changing economic, or even social or political, conditions? S. Prakash Sethi, Nobuaki Namiki and Carl L. Swanson argue that Japanese business must adjust to changing economic conditions. Japanese business leaders have been forced to rethink such basic practices as lifetime employment, seniority-based promotion and wage systems, and decision making by consensus. But employees were conditioned to believe that such practices were inviolable.[11]

The possibility of human manipulation in strong corporate cultures is a major problem. The "virtues" of employees in such a culture, e.g., loyalty, trust, commitment, hard work, may, in certain cases, be examples of pseudo-virtues; one may be guided by ignorance rather than *phronēsis* because the so-called virtues may be, in the context in which they are manifested, as harmful as they are beneficial. Harold J. Leavitt argues that managers want control over people's passions and identifications, and often the attempt to manage corporate cultures is merely an attempt to gain loyal, believing, and supportive workers who are, therefore, more easily controlled.[12] Robert Howard argues that emphasis on corporate culture entails "concentrating on worker motivation and morale and, in this way, [management can] win employee commitment to and participation in the corporation's goals for working life."[13] He suggests that emphasizing shared values and feelings and meaningful work may only be the latest ploys to control the workplace. There is a danger, for example, that workers may be manipulated to feel rather than to be more autonomous and responsible.

Given the above analysis, then, the virtues of some strong corporate cultures may be pseudo-virtues, in the Platonic sense. Even if one assumes that the virtues of the employees are required for the achievement of the corporation's goals (these goals, however, may not be truly beneficial to the firm), such so-called virtues may not be beneficial to the agent. Business virtues that are truly ethical, if Plato is correct, must be beneficial both to the agent and to those people affected by the agent's conduct.

I should think that besides the particular values instilled in employees by a specific American business culture, they are also nurtured by the values of American business culture in general. That is, there are values basic to American business, and to dismiss these values as unimportant to a particular firm is tantamount to remaining unconscious of the deep habits that underlie American business conduct. Therefore, as I have suggested in Chapter 1, an analysis of the values and character traits that have driven American business (and are still influential)—such as the one I have given in Chapters 2 and 3—is necessary before one can develop a defensible business ethic.

Ouchi (*Theory Z*), Pascale and Athos (*The Art of Japanese Management*), and Peters and Waterman (*In Search of Excellence*)[14] have been instrumental in popularizing the importance of the notion of corporate culture. In Chapter 6, we have seen that Peters and Waterman blame business managers for overemphasizing finance and generally short term bottom line concerns. Interestingly enough, they underscore the irony of calling a strictly bottom line approach to business ("the analytic approach") the "rational model." A truly rational model, they think, emphasizes knowledge of the values that ought to guide a firm. "While it is true that the good companies have superb analytic skills, we believe that their major decisions are shaped more by their values than by their dexterity with numbers."[15] Human beings are quite willing, if given the chance, to dedicate themselves to values one might consider noble.[16] In general, excellent companies create environments in which employees can develop their abilities and be treated with respect and dignity. In Chapter 6, I attempted to show that if business modifies its values and practices along the lines suggested by Peters and Waterman, assuming that this is done in a sincere rather than manipulative way, a more virtuous business organization (in a Platonic sense) would be possible.

NOTES

1. Terrence E. Deal and Allan A. Kennedy, *Corporate Cultures: The Rites and Rituals of Corporate Life* (Reading, Mass.: Addison-Wesley Pub. Co., 1982), p. 5.

2. Deal and Kennedy, p. 13.

3. Stanley M. Davis, *Managing Corporate Culture* (Cambridge, Mass.: Ballinger Pub. Co., 1984), p. 3.

4. Jay W. Lorsch, "Managing Culture: The Invisible Barrier to Strategic Change," *California Management Review* (Winter 1986): 104.

5. Charles O'Reilly, "Corporations, Culture, and Commitment: Motivation and Social Control in Organizations," *California Management Review* (Summer 1989): 14.

6. Richard T. Pascale, "The Paradox of 'Corporate Culture': Reconciling Ourselves to Socialization," *California Management Review* (Winter 1985): 34.

7. See, for example, Modesto A. Maidique, "Point of View: The New Management Thinkers," *California Management Review* (Fall 1983): 151–161.

8. John Dewey, *The Theory of the Moral Life*, intro. Arnold Isenberg (New York: Holt, Rinehart and Winston, 1960), p. VIII.

9. Dewey, p. 91.

10. Deal and Kennedy, p. 18.

11. S. Prakash Sethi, Nobuaki Namiki, Carl L. Swanson, "The Decline of the Japanese System of Management," *California Management Review* (Summer 1984): 35–45.

12. Harold J. Leavitt, *Corporate Pathfinders: Building Vision and Values into Organizations* (Homewood, Ill.: Dow-Jones-Irwin, 1986), p. 170.

13. Robert Howard, *Brave New Workplace* (New York: Viking Penguin, 1985), p. 119.

14. William G. Ouchi, *Theory Z: How American Business Can Meet the Japanese Challenge* (Reading, Mass.: Addison-Wesley, 1981). Richard T. Pascale and Anthony G. Athos, *The Art of Japanese Management: Applications for American Executives* (New York: Warner Books, 1981). Thomas J. Peters and Robert H. Waterman Jr., *In Search of Excellence: Lessons from America's Best-Run Companies* (New York: Harper and Row, 1982).

15. Peters and Waterman, p. 51.

16. Peters and Waterman speak of "beautiful goals," and Pascale and Athos, goals "beyond profit."

INDEX